A Garland Series

The English Stage
Attack and Defense 1577 - 1730

A collection of 90 important works
reprinted in photo-facsimile in 50 volumes

edited by
Arthur Freeman
Boston University

Tragi-Comoedia

by

John Rowe

with a preface
for the Garland Edition by

Arthur Freeman

Garland Publishing, Inc., New York & London

1973

Library of Congress Cataloging in Publication Data

Rowe, John, 1626-1677.
   Tragi-comoedia.

   (The English stage: attack and defense, 1577-1730)
   Reprint of the 1653 ed. printed by L. Lichfield for
H. Cripps, Oxford.
   1. Witney, Eng.--Theater disaster, 1653.
2. Sermons, English. I. Title. II. Series.
DA690.W83R68 1973   942.5'72   70-170430
ISBN 0-8240-0599-6

DA
690
.W83R68
1973

Preface

John Rowe (1626-1677) was a nonconformist well versed in patristic and classical scholarship, jurisprudence and philosophy, who graduated B.A. from the puritans' citadel of Emmanuel College, Cambridge, in 1646, and was subsequently incorporated B.A. at Oxford, admitted M.A. and elected a fellow of Corpus Christi by the age of twenty-three. His first preferment was as lecturer at Witney, in Oxfordshire, where on 3 February 1652/3 (not 1653/4, as Chambers, Elizabethan Stage, IV, 36, has it) the accident here described took place. A group of strolling players, "amateurs" from Stanton-Harcourt, had been acting the old comedy of Mucedorus (ascribed variously to Greene, Peele, Lodge, and even Shakespeare: cf. Tucker Brooke's Shakespeare Apocrypha) in a few nearby towns; at Witney, having been denied the town hall, they played it before three or four hundred stage-starved onlookers in an upstairs room of the inn. After the second act the floor

5

PREFACE

broke and six (not five, as in DNB*) of the spectators, but no actors, were killed — a curious Commonwealth echo of the larger disasters at Paris Garden (1583) and the "Fatal Vespers," adjacent to the Blackfriars Theatre (1623). Like preacher John Field before him, John Rowe seized on the catastrophe for a series of sermons, ascribing it to God's judgment on the play, the players, and the audience, to say nothing of the timbers of the inn.*

A good account of the book and the accident is given by Madan, Oxford Books, III, 25. Our reprint is prepared from a copy in the British Museum (698.e.3[7].), collating ¶⁴ *⁴ ¶¶²A-K⁴, with the interesting crude woodcut on *3ʳ. Wing R 2067; Madan 2221; Lowe-Arnott-Robinson 281.

February, 1973   A. F.

Tragi-Comædia.

BEING A

BRIEF RELATION

OF THE STRANGE, AND

Wonderfull hand of God

discovered at W I T N Y, in the
Comedy Acted there *February*
the third, where there were some
Slaine, many *Hurt,* with seve-
rall other *Remarkable*
P A S S A G E S.

Together with what was Preached in three
Sermons on that occasion from *Rom.* 1.18.

Both which
May serve as some Check to the Growing *Atheisme*
of the Present Age.

By
J O H N R O W E of C.C.C. in *Oxford ,* Lecturer in
the Towne of W I T N Y.

It is time for thee, Lord to work, for they have made voyd thy Law.
Psal. 119. 126.
Verily he is a God that judgeth in the Earth. Psal. 58. 11.

Ὁ μὲν ὢν Θεὸς αὐτὸς, ὕτε ὁρατὸς, ὕτε αἰσθητὸς ἀλλὰ λόγῳ κỳ νόῳ
θεωρητὸς. τὰ δ' ἔργα αὐτῆ, κỳ πρᾶξις ἐναργὲς τε, κỳ αἰσθητὰ
ἔστη πάντεσιν ἀνθρώποις. *Onatus apud Stobæum.*

O X F O R D,
Printed by L. L I C H F I E L D, For H E N R Y C R I P P S.
Anno Dom. 1 6 5 3.

TO
MY HONOVRED
and much beloved Friends,
the Inhabitants of the Towne,
& Parish of WITNY.

Dearely beloved in the LORD,

H E *publishing of these few Papers*, both the pre-cedent Narrative, *and the* ensuing Sermons *of right belong to You, and you may challenge them as your owne. Among you it was that these wonders of the Lord were seen, and upon you it was that the* Lord hath shewen himselfe marvelous. Doe not quarrell with the Almighty for setting you up as the publik Theatre whereon he would manifest his holynesse, justice, & other Attributes to the world. We are his Creatures, and it were enough if we could say no more, but It is his pleasure to have it so. Yet there is other reason why we should quiet, and compose our selves,

and

and ſhake off all thoughts, and reaſonings that are apt
to ariſe, ſaying as the Church doth. We will beare
the indignation of the Lord, becauſe we have ſin-
ned againſt him. Though you are the people that doe
only ſuffer, yet you are not they that are only aymed
at. The Lord hath ſpoken from heaven to the whole
Nation, by what he hath done amongſt you, and teſti-
fied by a clear and eminent ſtroake againſt the mon-
ſtrous unparraleld Atheiſme, irreligion, profaneſſe,
which is walking up and downe in all places.

Though the Lord hath began with you, yet he may
not end with you. If his dealing with you make not
others wiſe, their plagues may be farre greater then
yours have been; and if ſo, it will be a mercy that
you were correctedſo ſoone, and not ſuffered to goe
on in your ſinnes; which would have brought heavier
ſorrowes in the end. Amongſt you it was that theſe
meane Sermons had their riſe, which were not in the
leaſt intended for the Preſſe, when firſt they were
Preached. But the deſires of ſome amongſt you to
have written Coppies of them, the longings and im-
portunity of others to have them publiſhed, the good
of the Towne in generall (which might ſeeme to require a ſtāding, & laſting remēbrance of theſe things)
ſeemed to be ſome call to me for the publiſhing of
them. To which I may adde the conſideration of
ſome little good the Lord I hope was pleaſed to doe
by theſe plain and meane Sermons: the hearts of ſome
being a little awakened, and the affection of others
ſtirred, and raiſed, and ſome provoked to attend on
the word thereby. Which ſparks being of the Lords
owne kindling, I thought it my duty to keep them a-
liveasmuch as lay in me. I hope you will beare with

uuj

my rudeneſſe of ſpeech, and plain ſpeaking : the Lord
being my witneſſe, that it is not a pleaſure to me, to
make bare your nakedneſſe, or diſcover your ſhame,
my ayme only being, that you may lay to heart your
ſinnes, ſeek pardon for them, and reformation of them.
My care hath been as much as may be, to abſtain from
all perſonall reflections, and not to make uſe of any
ones Name, that I might not grieve the ſpirits of any
by making them publike to the world, although if I
had inſiſted on ſome particulars, the ſtory might have
been ſet forth with more advātage in the eyes of ſome.
Some enlargments there have been in the Sermons, &
ſome larger explications of a few Scriptures, it being
not poſſible within ſuch a ſcantling of time, as is al-
lotted, to ſpeake fully to all things. Yet this you will
find, you have ſcarce any materiall paſſage omitted of
what was Preached, and the Additions which are (I
hope) not altogether unprofitable or unneceſſary. Some
Notes are put into the Margin, which need not trouble
the leſſe skilfull Reader, all obſcurity being avoyded
in the body of the Sermons themſelves. My humble
deſire, and requeſt to you is, that you will not lay aſide
this little Book as ſoon as it comes into your hands,
though the things are mean and contemptible, if you
conſider the perſon, parts, and years of him that brings
them unto you, and the manner of his delivering
them; yet are they great, and of moment, if you conſider him that ſends them to you, ſo farre forth as the
mind of God is revealed in them, and his particular
will made known concerning you. Some few houres
will ſerve to Reade over the whole Book, and if at
leaſure times, you put your Children or Servants to
reade but a little, it may be better then to let it lye

¶ 3   moulding

moulding in your Windows. Possibly you may meet with such a remembrance, if the Lord work with it by his Spirit, as yon may blesse him for all your dayes. I can only say as the Apostle doth with a little change. Brethren my hearts desire, and prayer to God for the people of *Witny* is, that they may be saved. I trust the Lord hath some of his election yet scattered amongst you, sure I am there are some of his called, and faithfull ones already to be found in the middest of you. How long I may be left to speak to you, I know not. This I can asure you, I pray, and sigh at the throne of Grace for you, as well as I can. And I could wish I had better prayers, and more sighs and groanes, then my poore barren heart can afford. There could not be a greater joy to me, then to see the Kingdome of our Lord Jesus taking place in greater power in your soules: to see that high valuation, and eager thirsts in the hearts of many of you after a poore despised, neglected, forsaken Christ, whom the world (but it may break our hearts to speak it) begins to grow weary of, though the world be not worthy of such a one.

Now the God and Father of our Lord Jesus blesse you with the knowledge of himselfe, and this his deare Sonne, and grant that the favour of his knowledge may be spread amongst you more abundantly. These are the constant prayers of

Your unworthy Friend, and Servant,

in the Gospell

John Rowe.

A BRIEFE

NARRATIVE OF
The Play Acted at *Witny* the
third of *February* 1652. Together
with its sad and Tragicall End.

IT may not seem so proper , nor be so plea-
sing to every Reader , to set down all the
Circumstances about this *Play* , forasmuch
that somewhat might be said touching the
rise and originall of it , the nature of the
Play it self, and the book from whence it was taken ,the motives,grounds,and ends of the Actors,
concerning all which I might speak more then
here shall be inserted , having taken some paines
to satisfie my selfe in those particulars. But I
thought it meet to insist on those things, which
did most discover the hand of God in so eminent
and remarkable a Providence , and lightly touch
on other things , so far as they may give light to
that

that which is the name. This *Play* was an old *Play*, and had been Acted by some of *Santon-Harcourt* men many years since. The Title of it is, *A most pleasant Comedy of* Mucedorus *the Kings Sonne of Valentia*, *and* Amadine *the Kings Daughter of Aragon* : *with the merry conceits of* Mouse, &c. The Actors of the *Play* were Countreymen; most of them, and for any thing I can heare, all of *Stanton- Harcourt* Parish. The punctuall time of their first Learning the *Play*, cannot be certainly set downe: but this we have been told, they had been learning it ever since *Michaelmas*, and had been Acting privatly every week. This we are informed upon more certain grounds, that they began to Act it in a more publike manner about *Christmas*, and Acted it three or foure times in their own Parish, they Acted it likewise in severall neighbowring Parishes, as *Moore, Stanlake, South-Leigh, Cumner*. The last place that they came at was *Witny*, where it pleased the Lord to discover his displeasure, against such wicked and ungodly *Playes* by an eminent hand. Some few dayes before the *Play* was to be Acted, one of *Stanton* came to the *Baylife* of *Witny* telling him *that there were some Countrey men that had learn'd to make a Play*, and desired his Leave to shew it, his aime being (as the *Baylife* conceiv'd) that they might have the Liberty of the *Towne-Hall.* Leave also was desired of the other *Baylife*, but they being denied by both the *Baylifs*, they pitched on the *White Hart*, a chiefe Inne of the Towne to Act their *Play* there. The day when it was Acted, was the third of *February*

bruary, the same day when many Godly People, Townesmen and Schollars of *Oxford*, kept a Solemne Day of *Fast* at *Carfax*. About seaven a Clock at Night they caused a Drum to beat, and a Trumpet to be sounded to gather the People together. The people flocked in great multitudes, Men, Women, and Children, to the number (as is guefs'd) of three Hundred, some say foure hundred, and the Chamber where the *Play* was Acted being full, others in the Yard preffed sorely to get in. The people which were in the Roome were exceeding Joviall, and merry before the *Play* began, Young men and Maides dancing together, and so merry and frolick were many of the Spectators, that the Players could hardly get Liberty that they themselves might Act, but at laft a little Liberty being obtained, the *Play* it felf began. In the beginning of it Enters a Perfon that took the name of Comedie, and fpeaks as follows.

Why fo thus doe I hope to pleafe,
Muficke revives, and Mirth is tolerable,
Comedie *play thy part, and pleafe:*
Make merry them that come to joy with thee.
With two or three verfes more.
Vpon this enters *Envy*, another perfon, & fpeaks as followes.

Nay ftay Minion ftay there lyes a block;
What all on mirth? I'le interrupt your tale,
And mix your Muficke with a Tragick end.
Vpon which *Comedie* replyes. *Envy* makes anfwer againe in feverall verfes, and among the reft thefe.

*

Harken

Harken thou shalt heare noyse
Shall fill the ayre with shrilling sound,
And thunder Musick to the Gods above.
Three verses after it followes,
In this brave Musick Envy takes delight
Where I may see them wallow in their bloud,
To spurne at Armes & Leggs quite shivered off,
And heare the cryes of many thousand slaine.
After this *Comedie* speaks, *Envy* replies
--Trebble death shall crosse thee with dispight,
And make thee mourn where most thou joyest,
Turning thy mirth into a deadly dole,
Whirling thy pleasurs with a peale of death,
And drench thy methods in a Sea of bloud.

Which passages if the Reader carry along with
him, he will see how farre they were made good
by the Divine hand, both on the Actors and Spectators. The matter of the *Play* is scurrilous, im-
pious, blasphemous in severall passages. One passage of it hath such a bitter Taunt against all *God-*
ly persons under the name of *Puritans*, and at *Reli-*
gion it selfe, under the phrase *of observing Fasting*
days, that it may not be omitted, it was almost in
the beginning of the *Play*, and they were some of
the Clownes words when he first began to Act,
Well Ile see my Father hang'd before Ile serve his
Horse any more, well Ile carry home my bottle of Hay
and for once make my Fathers Horse turne Puritan,
and observe Fasting dayes, for he gets not a bitt. How
remarkable was this that some of them that were
called *Puritans* in the dayes of old, had spent that
very

very day in *Oxford* in Fasting , and Prayer; and
that the Lord by so eminent an hand should testi-
fie against such , who were not only scoffers at
Godly persons , but at *Religion* it selfe. Another
passage was of so horrid an aspect , as that the A-
ctor who was to speak it durst not vent it without
a change. The verses as they are Printed are these.
Ah Bremo, Bremo, *what a foyle hadst thou,*
that yet at no time was afraid
To dare the greatest Gods to fight with thee
At the end of which verses it followeth, *He*
strikes: and probable enough it is, that he used
some action at that time; but the words were so
gastly, and had such a face of impiety in them,
that he durst not say *Gods,* but (as one that excu-
sed him would have us believe)he sai'd *Gobs.* And
indeed so insolent were these, and other expressions in the Play , that some of the Spectators
thought they were not fit to be used, and when
they heard them, wished themselves out of the
roome. We might instance in some other passages,
but there hath been enough already. The modest,
and ingenuous reader would blush to read some
passages. Thus had they continued their sport for
an hour, and halfe,as some of the Spectators say,
but as is more probable, about two houres, for
they were ordinarily three houres in acting it (as
the Players say) and there were aboue two parts
in three of the play that were passed over in this
Action. At which time it pleased God to put a stop
to their mirth, and by an immediate hand of his
owne, in causing the chamber to sink, and fall
under

under them, to put an end to this ungodly Play
before it was thought, or intended by them.

The Actors who were now in action were *Bremo*
a wild man, (courting, and folliciting his Lady,
and among other things, begging a *Kiſſe* in this
verſe.

Come kiſſe me (Sweet) for all my
favours paſt)

And *Amadine* the Kings daughter (as named in
the Play) but in truth a young man attired in a
womans Habit. The words which were then
ſpeaking, were theſe, the words of *Bremo* to his
Lady.

Thou ſhalt be fed with Quailes, and Partridges,
With Black-birds, Larkes, Thruſhes,
and Nightingales.

Various reports there have been concerning
the words ſpoken at that time, as that it ſhould
be ſayed, *the Devill was now come to act his part:*
ſome of the People might ſay ſo, obſerving the
wild mans carriage, and ſome other paſſages that
went before, where there was mention made of
the Divell in a Bares dublet, the *wild man* then
acting the Bares part: and indeed we have it upon good information that there were ſuch words
ſpoken; only they were the *ſpectators* words, and
not the *Actors*: but this we are aſſured of, the
words then ſpoken by the *Actor* were thoſe above
mentioned, as *he himſelfe* acknowledged, and we
find them printed ſo in the Book.

The *Place* wherein the *Play* was acted , was not
a *Stage* erected on purpoſe, but a *Chamber* belong-
ing

ing to the *Inne*, a larg Chamber, and which fometime had been a Malting roome, having a part of it covered with earth to that purpofe. It had two Beames to fupport it, of which one Sc: the fhorter was a great, foūd & fubftantiall one, & lay between the two fide walls; the other had one end fhooting into the middle of the fhorter beame, and the other end of it faftned in the wall, of which you may fee a defcription.

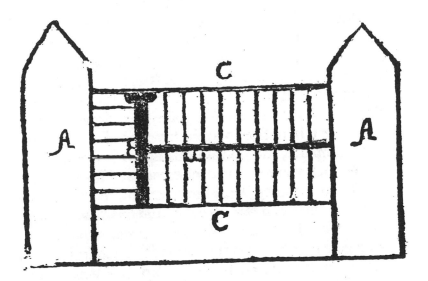

The 2 end Walls. A. The 2 Beames B. The fid- Walls C. The fhort Beame, which broke neare the middle, was betwixt 13 and 14 Inches fquare, one end lying even, or a little within the Wall upon a fhoulder of Stone, the other end almoft a foot in the Wall, the fhort Beame breaking, the other fell with it.

The

The fall was not very quick, but somewhat
flow, & gentle, in so much that foe that were prefent thought it was a part of the play, (but it proved the faddeft part) & expected whe they fhould
be taken up againe, yet was it not fo flowe as that
they were able to recover themfelves, for the actors then in action fell down, and a great number
of people with them into the under roome, which
was a *Shufle-board-roome*, and the *table* it felfe broken in peeces by the fall of the Timber. The
Chamber did not fall down quite, but lay fomewhat pendulous, and hanging, broad at the top,
and narrow at the bottome, that end of the
long beame, which lay in the fhort falling down,
the other end not falling, & the ends of the fhort
Beame where it brake hanging down, the
bottome where the people lay was of a very narrow compaffe, the people falling as it were into a
Pit: & fuch were the apprehentions of fome of the
Spectators, feeing the chamber fink in that manner as if the *earth was opening, and fwallowing them
up.* After the Crack of the beame which was
exceeding great, and the fall of the Chamber (in
the manner as is before defcribed) all was quiet,
and ftill, and a kind of filence for a pretty fpace
of time; the people being aftonied, and bereft of
their fenfes. One that was prefent was fo much
affrighted (as was faid) that fhe thought her felfe
verily to be in Hell, which we do the rather infert
becaufe whoever fhall put the circumftances together may well fay it was a little refemblance of
that black, and difmall place, there being fo many

ny taken in the middeſt of their ſinfull practiſes, and thruſt into a pit together where they were left in darkneſſe, the *Lights* being put out by the fall, where the duſt that was raiſed made a kind of Miſt, and Smoake, where there were the moſt lamentable ſkreekes, and out-cryes that may be imagined; where they were ſhut up as in a priſon, and could not get themſelves out, (the doore of the under roome being blocked up, and their leg's being ſo pinioned, & wedged together by faggots, and other things, that fell down together with them from the upper roome, that they could not ſtirre to help themſelves.) Another (as is ſaid) ſuppoſing his limbs to be all plucked aſunder cryed out, *that they ſhould cut off his head:* this is certaine, the fright was exceeding great , and many were dead for a time that afterward came to themſelves. When the people were come to themſelves, there was a fearfull, and moſt lamentable cry, ſoe crying one thing, ſoe another, ſome crying *aid for the Lords ſake,* others *crying Lord have mercy on us* , *Chriſt have mercy on us,* others cryed oh my Huſband! a ſecond , oh my Wife! a third , Oh my child! and another ſaid, No body loves *me* ſo well as to ſee where my child is. Others cryed out for Ladders, and Hatchets to make their paſſage out, for the chamber falling, the doore of the under roome was ſo Blocked up that they could not get out there, ſo that they were fain to break the barres of the window , and moſt of the people got out that way though it were a good ſpace of time before
they

they could get forth. The other Players that were not in action were in the Attiring-roome which was joyning to the chamber that fell, and they helped to fave fome of the people which were neer that part. Thofe of the people that fell not down, but were preferved by that meanes got out at the window of the upper roome. There were five flaine outright, whereof three were Boys, two of which being about feaven, or eight yeares old or thereabout; the other neer twelve: the other two were Girles, the elder of which being fourteen, or fiveteen, and the younger twelve, or thirteen yeares old. A woman alfo had her legg forely broken that the furgeons were forced to cut it off, and fhe dyed within three or foure dayes after it was cut off. Many were hurt, and forely bruifed, to the number of about threefcore, that we have certaine information of, befides thofe that conceale their greifes, and fome of the Contry of which there were diverfe prefent, it being market day when this Play was acted..

The Surgeon that dreffed the wounded people, told me that the next day after this was done he was counting with himfelfe how many he had dreffed, and as neere as he could reckon he had dreffed about fortie five, and twelve after that as he had fuppofed, and two or three after he had cut off the womans legg. Which therefore I thought good to infert that the reader may know upon what grounds he may take this relation.

Some others were dreffed by others in the town

the

the juſt number of which I have not learn't But it is generally conceaved that there were divers did receive hurt which would not ſuffer it to be knowen. Among thoſe that were hurt there were about a dozen broken armes, and leggs, and ſome two or three diſlocations, as we were likewiſe informed by the Surgeon. Some of the people came out with bloody faces, neither could it be otherwiſe, they having trod one upon another in a moſt ſad, and lamentable manner. Certain it is there was much hurt done that way; the children that were killed, being ſtifled as was ſuppoſed. The man in womans apparrell lay panting for breath, and had it not been for *Bremo* his fellow Actor, he had been ſtifled; but *Bremo* having recovered himſelfe a little, bare up the others head with his arme, whereby he got ſome breath, and ſo was preſerved; but both the one, and the other were hurt; *Bremo* being ſo ſorely bruiſed, as that he was fain to keep his bed for two dayes after, and the Lady had her beuty mar'd, her face being ſwoln by the hurt taken in the fall. Some had their mouths ſo ſtuf'd with duſt that they could hardly ſpeak, the people that came from the houſe made a pittifull moane, ſome going in the ſtreets, and complaining, here is a Play, a ſad Play indeed, others crying out to them that met them, (as they are wont that have received ſome deadly wound)oh I am kil'd! Some cryed out that their Armes were broken, others that their Leggs were broken, ſome curſed the Players that ever they came to *Witny*, and the players them-

¶ ¶   ſelves

felves wifhed that they had never came thither.
They that received no hurt were exceedingly affrighted, infomuch that one of them that were
prefent, as I am credibly informed, did fay, that
he would not, for as much as *Witny* was worth, be
in the like affright again, though he were fure he
fhould have no hurt. Others faid they would never goe to a play more, and that it was a judgment. Others have been fo prophane; as we hear,
to make a laughing-ftock of it, and fome fo defpe-
rate, as to fay, they would go againe, if it were to
morrow next: and too many apt to fay it was but
a chance, a misfortune, the beame was weak, there
were fo many load of people there, and the like.
But how fleight fo ever the matter was made af-
terwards, fure enough it is, it was fad enough
then. It was one of the faddeft, and blackeft nights
that ever came on *Witny*. Sad it was to fee Parents carry home their Children dead in their
armes, fad it was to fee fo many bruifed, hurt, and
maimed, and fome, as it were, halfe-dead that
were not able to help themfelves, but were fain to
be carryed away by their friends, fome on their
backs, fome on chaires, fad it was to hear the pit-
teous cryes of thofe that were not there bemoa-
ning their diftreffed friends. This was the fad end
of this ungodly play. And what was fpoken in jeft
in the beginning of it, by the juft hand of God,
was made good in earneft. The Comedy being
turned into a Tragedy, it had a fad *Cataftrophe*,
ending with the deaths of fome, and hurts of many. And as it was faid before

And

And make thee mourn where most thou
joy'st
    So by the just hand of God came it to passe. For in the midst of their mirth, and jollity did this fall out, in the middest of these amorous passages between *Bremo*, and his Lady was this stroke given; yea, immediately before they expected the greatest pleasure, and contentment. For the Actors said the best of the play was still behind, and a little after the hearts, and fancyes of the Spectators were to be filled with the love-complements between *Mucedorus*, and his *Amadine*. So true was that

    Turning thy mirth into a deadly Dole.

    The Lord from heaven, having given a check to such wanton sports, teaching men what they must look for, and that he will not bear with such grosse open profanenesse in such an age of light as this is. That he will so farre take notice of the Atheisme, and profanenesse of men in this world, as shall keep the world in order, though he hath reserved the great, and full recompence for another day, and place.

ROM. I. XVIII.

For the wrath of God is revealed from heaven againſt all ungodlineſſe, and unrighteouſneſſe of men, who hold the truth in unrighteouſneſſe.

IT may ſeeme ſtrange to The Preface. ſome of you to heare ſuch a text read. What, is love ſo ſoone turned into wrath? The laſt time I was called to ſpeak unto you upon a Lords day, the firſt words of the text were *God is love;* 1 Joh 4. 8. 9. pure love, goodneſſe, and ſweetneſſe, all love as it were, made up of love. Now the text beginnes with *the wrath of God,* heavy wrath, dreadfull, aſtoniſhing wrath: enough to break in pieces the hardeſt heart to heare it but ſo much as mention'd. Its the wrath of *God;* Its wrath *from heaven,* its *revealed wrath,* tis mani-feſted, and declared in open ſight. This is a great

A   change

change indeed may fome one fay to paffe from the fweeteft Love to the moft terrible and difmall wrath. But the Lord himfelfe hath changed the text, and it is he that hath given it, by that which he hath wrought in the midft of you, and done in the face of the whole Towne. Can you look back upon that late fad and aftonifhing Providence, of which as many as heare, their eares tingle at it, their hearts fhake and tremble at it:can you, I fay, look upon this ftrange & wonderfull Providence, and not fee this written in Broad and Capitall letters , and even laid before you in what is come to paffe. *That the wrath of God is revealed from heaven againft all ungodlineffe, and unrighte-oufneffe of men.*

Be not prejudiced, my Brethren, doe not miftake me:I am not come to grate upon your foares, neither to make wider your yet bleeding wounds: God forbid ; no, I pitty and pray for thofe among you, that are yet weake and infirme, befeeching the Lord to heale them, and reftore them, that they may live to teftify their thankfulneffe, and Repentance. My work is, as a poor unworthy Embaffadour, and fervāt of the Lord, to help you to underftand what the meaning of the Lord is; for certainly fo great a thing could not be in vaine. *The Lords voice crieth unto the citie,* faith the Prophet Micah.6. 95 *And the man of wifdome fhall fee thy Name:beare ye the rod, and who hath appointed it.* There is a voice gone out to you of this place, and it is the Lords voice, his Name is written upon what was done but the other week, this name

of

of his is wrirten with faire and legible charaters, that he which runnes may read: this voice of his, it doth not whifper,it doth not mutter,no, it *cries*, it fpeakes aloud, it will be your wifdome to heare this voice. Every rod hath a voice in it, the mea- neft and moft petty afflitions fpeak fomething from God. Great and mighty ftrokes, eminent and remarkable Judgments from heaven, they have a loud voice, and if fuch be not heard, they bring fpeedy ruine.

Let not any among you fay, the Preacher is come to vent himfelfe, and his own Paffions, and we expeted fome thundering fermon after this: No, no, I am not come to that purpofe, but in all humility and ferioufneffe to befeech you to confi- der what the mind of the Lord is, and I have beg'd from the Lord (as well as I could) wifedome and diretion to know what I fhould fpeak : be not fuch enemies to your felves, and to that good the Lord intends you this day, as to fay when you come home,we have heard a fermõ of Judgment, and that is all; we expeted fome fuch thing. Do not fo ill requite the Lord and his word, but har- ken to the counfels of his word,and be obedient to the fame.

The fcope of the Apoftle in this Epiftle, is to fet downe the true way of mens Juftification, and fal- vation; which he affirmes to be by the pure grace of God, and not by the works of men. This way, or modell of God in faving men, the materi- all principle from whence both their Juftification and Salvation muft arife, *viz imputed righteouf-*

The Cohe- rence.

A 2   *neffe,*

neſſe, he calls the *righteouſneſse of God* in the verſe
before the text, which is ſo called, becauſe the
righteouſneſſe by which men are ſaved is a
righteouſneſſe of Gods finding out, and of his own
beſtowing, and not any ſuch thing as men have either framed, and deviſed themſelves;or were able
to work out by any thing that they could doe.
This righteouſneſſe, he ſaies, is revealed in the
Goſpell: it is the Goſpell that chalkes out this modell, and plat-forme of righteouſneſſe and life, and
by this way muſt men be juſtified and ſaved, and
not by their owne workes: this is the maine propo-
ſition which he layes down in the 17 verſe. In the
text we have the firſt proof, or argument to make
that aſſertion good,& the argument ſtands thus.

The workes of all men in the world, whether
Jewes or Gentiles, ever ſince the fall of Adam, they
are wicked, ungodly, unrighteous workes, therefore they cannot be ſaved by them: the argument
is very cleare, and ſtrong here. All men deſerve
wrath, the utmoſt wrath, diſpleaſure, and vengeance of God by their owne workes, therefore they
cannot deſerve his love, favour, or good will: they
are ſo far from deſerving his love, that they deſerve the quite contrary. This is the coherence.

For explication of the words,

The wrath of God]By *wrath,* we are to underſtand wrath in the Root, and in the Fruit; in the
caufe, and in the effect. God is highly diſpleaſed
with men by reaſon of ſin, he loathes their wayes
and abhorres their practiſes, he beares a bitter, and
a deadly hatred againſt all the wickedneſſe which
men

The open-
ing of the
Text.

men commit; and he hath an inward quarrell,(if we may fo fpeak) a fecret grudge in his heart a-gainft men themfelves for the fame: this is wrath in the root, or caufe. And then againe he inflicts plagues and punifhments, the moft dreadfull cur-fes, and fearfull judgments on men by reafon of fin; all which are vifible and fignall tokens of his difpleafure, and manifeft proofs, that he cannot endure them, nor any of their wayes: this is wrath in the fruit, or effect.

Is revealed from heaven.

There may be a twofold fenfe of this.

1. The fenfe may be,it is revealed clearly and manifeftly, as much as if it were by a voice from heaven. The Lord God Almighty, the bleffed and moft holy God, he proclaimes it from heaven,and cries aloud in the eares of all the world, that he is deeply offended with all the ungodlineffe,and un-righteoufneffe which men cōmit,that he will cer-tainly call them to an account, and punifh them for it. In *Pfalm*: 14. 2. it is faid:*The Lord looked from* HEAVEN *upon the children of men, to fee if there were any that did underftand, and feek God;* now here it is faid, his wrath is revealed *from hea-ven.* God is no idle fpectator, he doth not care-lefly behold the actions of men, as if fo be they might doe what they lifted, and he not difcerne, or not be moved at it: no, he looks down from heaven *upon the children of men.* Jehovah from the heavens looked down upon the fons of *Adam*; fo one reads it: He looks with a watchfull obfer-vant eye;his eye is intent and fixt upon all the fons

a 'Aπ' ἐρανϖ
e cælo.
Simpliciter
fignificat Pau
lus,manifefti-
us effe quam
ut quifquam
inficiari po-
ffit,Dominum
e cælo in om-
nes ac fingu-
los homines
indignari.
Beza..

A 3　　　　　of

of *Adam*.upon the whole raceof mankind,and for
what is all this curious fearch made *?* it is *to fee
if there were any that did underſtand and feek God*:
But was he well pleafed when he found it otherwife? no furely, finding all to be *corrupt*, that they
were *all gone aſide*,that *they were* all together *becōe
filthy*,that *there was none that did good no not one*,
that they were *workers of* iniquity.v. 1.3.4.he gives
out the fentence,he pronoūceth it *from heaven*, he
proclaimes it in the eares of all the world, that he
is highly offended, and his wrath is gone out a-
gainſt men by reafon of thefe things. Pfalm: 4. 2.
*O ye fons of men how long will ye love vanity,
and feek after leafing?* how long will ye run
mad on fin, and be fo defperately adventerous in
the waies in which you walk? *But know that the
Lord hath fet apart him that is godly for himfelfe*.
verfe 3: Take it for granted, that JEHOVAH,
that is,the HigheſtLord,the Majeſty of heaven and
earth, he is provoked, and incenfed by all thefe
waies,and it is the godly-man that he lookes after:
know ye, Jehovah hath marveloufly feperated a
gratious faint to him; *fo Ainfworth*. It is the pious,
devout, holy foul that Jehovah regards, and he
hath marveloufly feperated him, or felected in
wondrous fort, b he hath put him in another
rank, fet a mark of excellency upon him,he hath
fet him in oppofition to the wicked ungodly men,
and fuch as love vanity, whome he hath fet on
another file, whofe names are written in his black
book, and hath marked them out as the objects
of his wrath. this is illuſtrated *Pfal.* 11. 4: 5: *ver.*

b *fegregavit,
Græcun, &
Latinum, mi-
rificavit*, quod
verbum non
eſt alienum a
propofito ubi
bi de opilio-
ne ad regiam
dignitatem e.

The

The Lord is in his holy temple, The Lords throne is in heaven: his eyes behold, his eye-lids tries the children of men.

The Lord trieth the righteous: but the wicked, and him that loveth violence his soul hateth.

Another *sense* may be , the wrath of God is *revealed from heaven,* that is, it is manifested by evident, cleare, remarkable plagues,and Judgments *from heaven.* God hath discovered to all the world, that he is an utter enemy to all the sin, wickednesse, and ungodlinesse of men, because he hath punished in all generations wicked, and ungodly men with most fearfull plagues and judgments; he hath shewen signes, and tokens *from heaven,* so that all men have seene his hand. A learned expositor understands this phrase from *Heaven,* as that which is opposed to the opinion of prophane men, who ascribe the punishments that are ever now and then lighting upon men, to chance, or second causes, the position of the starres, the malignity of the elements, the mutability of the matter: whereas the Apostle shewes clearly that this wrath descēds from heaven,and is even the *scourge* and *whip of God,* whereby he revengeth the impiety and injustice of the world.

Against all ungodlinesse, and unrighteousnesse of men: by *ungodlinesse,* we are to understand sinnes against the first Table , all contempt of God, of religion, of the worship of God, of the waies and ordinances of God, the wrong and injury that is done to God himself more immediately, or to any part of his worship. [d]

vecto agitur; neq; a , Grammatica, cùm verba , quæ *mirabile facere & separare* Hebraice significant, fimilia fint, atque idcirco fuas fignificatiões facile confundere poffint ex regula Grammaticorum, & ufu Hebraicæ linguæ. Muis in loc.

Parcus.

[d] Ἀσέβεια ἀδικία ἐι᾽ τὸ θεῖον.

By Phav.

By *unrighteoufneffe* is mean't fins againft the fecond Table, all oppreffion, injuftice, riot, exceffe; and the like.

Againft *all* ungodlineffe, and unrighteoufneffe becaufe there are feverall fins comprehended under either head

Here alfo *ungodlineffe* and *unrighteoufneffe* is put for perfons committing fuchthings,the Abftract being put for the Concrete. *Who hold the truth &c.*

This is added as an aggravation of the finne of men, that men fin againft light and knowledge, and therefore doe more abundantly deferve that wrath which is reveal'd from heaven againft them. The doctrine arifing hence is this.

Doctrine   *The Bleffed, and moft holy God hath all along manifefted, and declared his utter hatred, abhorrence, and deteftation of all ungodly, and unrighteous perfons; and of all the ungodlineffe and unrighteouneffe which they commit: and at fundry times hath confirm'd, and made good that difpleafure of his by fearfull, and terrible Judgments inflicted on men in this world.*

Or more briefly that you may all remember it. *God is certainly angry with fin, and finners, and doth oftentimes in this world fhew his difpleafure againft them by remarkable Judgments.*

In the profecution of this we muft fhew

1. what this *hatred*, or *wrath* of God meaneth.

2. Prove in a fcripture or two,that this wrath of God fo opened, and unfolded hath been manifefted to have been in God.

3. how, or by what wayes, and meanes it hath been manifefted.

4. Give proof, that it hath been confirm'd by

Judgments

Judgments inflicted on men from time to time.

5. Why God takes this course to manifest his wrath by plagues, and judgments in this world.

1. What is this wrath of God?

It implyeth two things: the Holinesse of his will: the Justice of his will.

1. The *Holinesse of his will*: the will of God is absolutely, universally set against all sin, he dislikes it, he abhorres it, he hates it to the very death, it is that which goes against him, he cannot endure it, neither will he, it strikes at his own blessednesse, & therefore he must needs hate it. [f] Heb. 1. 9. *Thou hast loved righteousnesse, and hated iniquity.* That, which a man hateth, he wisheth the death of. God hath taken up an irreconcileable, and eternall hatred against sin, it never stood with his holinesse to like it, neither ever will it. Nay; he is so holy he cannot but hate it. The wrath of God therefore is the displeasure, which he hath conceived in his heart against sin, the secret grudge, and quarrell which he beares to every man that is a sinner, and cannot but beare to him considered as such, and remaining in that estate. [g] Wrath, as the Philosophers define it, is a desire of revenge for some seeming sleight, or disrespect shewen to a man. As a Prince when he is disgraced, reviled, reproched or any way struck at by one of his subjects, [h] he is presently inflamed, his blood is up, [i] & he resolves to right himselfe, and to revenge the quarrell of his honour on such a man. But God hath no such passions, only so far we may say, the blessed God looks upon sin as a sleight, as a disrespect shewen unto him he looks upō

B   sin and

[f] Omne impediens à beatitudine debet odiri. Aquin.

[g] Ἡ ὀργή ὄρεξίς τιμωρίας διά φαινομένην ὀλιγωρίαν. Aristot.

[h] Sola parvipensio causat iram, & omne provocans iram est aliquid sub ratione injusti. Aquin.

[i] Ira est ζῆσις ὀρεγδιν αἵμαϊ@- δι᾽ ὄρεξιν ἀντιλυπήσεως. Eustratius referent. Grot.

'Οργὴ ἐσιν
ἐπιθυμία
πρὸς τὸ τιμω-
ρήσαθχ τ̃ δb.
κῦντα ἢ δι-
κηκέναι παρὰ
τὸ προῆκον·
Phavor.

and finners as contemning his holy majefty , as fcorning him, and fetting him at nought, and this he hates, and cannot but hate.

2. The k wrath of God implyes the *juftice* of his will, the will of God hates fin, and it is refolved to punifh fin, the will of God is carried with utter dif- like of fin, and it will be reveng'd for fin, it will in-

* Est autem
pæna genera-
li significatu
malum passi-
onis quod
infligitur ob
malum ac-
tionis. Gro-
tius de jure
belli& pacis.

flict punifhment for fin. Wrath in our fenfe is a de- fire of revenge, when there is fome evill inflicted proportionable to the wrong a man fuffers, and this is properly-called punifhment.* Now there are no paffions in God, as was faid before, but thus we muft conceive it; God refolves to lay a meet re-

Δικαίωμα
Θεῦ. jus
Dei.

compence, a juft reward upon men for fin; fin in its own nature, deferves the heavieft curfes, and therefore thefe are meafured out by the juft, and upright will of God, as the fitteft recompence

k Ad jus au-
tem pertinet
aptitudo
quam Aristo-
teles. ἀξίαν
id est dig-
nitatem vo-
cat. Michael
Ephesius id
quod secun-
dum eam æ-
quale dicitur
interpreta-
tur τὸ πρὸς
ἀρμόζον ἢ τὸ
πρέπον quod
convenit.
Grotius de
jure belli &
pacis.

thereunto.

This is the judgment of God, that they which com- mit fuch things are k worthy of death. Rom. 1. 32. *God will render to every man according to his workes.* Chap. 2. 6. This is another thing that muft be un- derftood by the wrath of God, the diftributive juftice of God whereby he lay's actuall plagues, and punifhments on men according to their deferts. Pfalm. 2. 5. *Then fhall he fpeak unto unto them in his wrath, and vex them in his fore difpleafure.* Here is wrath, and the fruit of wrath; the Lord is angry, and he makes it known that he is fo; his an- ger is a vexing, troubling anger, it leaves not men at eafe in their finnes, but it quickly difquiets them.

The

2. The Second particular for the profecuting of the doctrine, was to inftance in a Scripture or two, whereby it apeares that there is fuch anger in God towards fin, and finners;and to proove that there is fuch wrath indeed, which hath been manifefted as hanging over men by reafon of fin. One or two places will be enough for this. *Ezra.8.22. The hand of our God is upon all them for good that feek him, but his power, and his wrath is againft all them that forfake him. Nahum. 1. 2. God is jealous, and the Lord revengeth ; the Lord revengeth, and is furious; the Lord will take vengeance on his adverfaries, and he referveth wrath for his enemies.* The Prophet is here defcribing the nature of God,and he beginnes with jealoufy.

1 Jealoufy is an affection proceeding frō ftrength, and intenfnes of love, and that which ftirres it up is fomewhat that would rob a man of the quiet,and fole enjoyment of what he defires. God loves himfelfe and his own glory above all, and good reafon for it , he being the higheft and moft fupreme good.Sin in its proper nature, and intention goes about to rob him of what is neareft to him and therefore no wonder if he be jealous. This jealoufy of his is manifefted in the next wordes, *The Lord revengeth, the Lord revengeth, the Lord taketh vengeance.* m The name of Jehovah is thrice repeated in this one verfe,this he doth to fhew that it is the true,and living God,he that is omnipotent, whofe power and wrath none can refift, that was fallen out with them , and become their enemie. And n the name of vengeance is as oftē attributed

1 Aquinas. 1ma: 2dæ. Quæft. 28. Art: 4.

m Cum vero ait Dominus femper eft in Heb: יהוה, ut intelligant Deum verum, & omnipotentē fibi effe iratum, qui nullius potentiâ prohiberi,auc impediri poffit. Ribera.

n Ter antem ulcifcens, five

vltor dicitur, quod asseve-rationem magnam ha-bet, maxi-mumq; in di-cat,& certissi-mam ultio-nem:etenim *Ternarius* magnam vim habet ad amplifican-dum. *Ribera.*

o Dominum iræ vocat, ira & indignati-one prædi-tum q.d.non-nunquam of-tendit se esse iratum, quū infligit gra-ves pœnas. *Vatabl.*

p Ego חמה non Simpli-citer accipio pro irâ sed pro effectu iræ. *Calv. in loc.*

q Πῦ παρέ-βλω;τῆ δ' ἔ-ρεξα,ἤμοι δέον ἐκ ἐτε-λήθη. *Pyth. aur.car.* Διχῶς γδ ἁ-μαρτάνομεν, ἤ τὸ μὴ δέον ποιῶντες, ὁ διὰ τῦ πρέβλω δυλῦ) ἤ τὸ μὴ δέον ποιῶσαντες, ὡς ἐπ' αὐτῆς κῆται λέξεως. *Sic Hierocles in versum.*

to him,the Lord *revengeth,revengeth, will take ven-geance*,which shewes the terriblenesse of his wrath, and the certainty of it. There are also two other expressions that set forth the greatnesse, and cer-tainty of his wrath, *he is furious*, or as the Margin hath it *that hath fury*,which best suits with the Ori-ginall which hath it,° the *Lord of Anger*,that is,one that is armed with wrath, and indignation against his enemies, & shewes himself to be angry by infli-cting grievous punishments on thē. p *Calvin* there-fore understands the Hebrew word signifying *fury* or *anger*, not of anger or wrath simply,but of the effect of anger : and whereas 'tis said that he is the *Lord of anger*, or he *possesseth* anger,it imports, that he is armed with revenge, and that he holds anger in his hand, which in due time he powreth on the heads of his enimies.p This is intimated in the other expression, *he reserveth wrath for his enemies*. The word wrath is not againe repeated in the originall, but is taken from that which went before to make the sense compleat.He is the Lord of wrath, he hath plagues & punishmēts enough at his cōmand: these he reserves & keepes by him for a fit time,& then,be sure, he will execute them to the utmost. 3. *The third Particular*. By what wayes,and meanes hath this wrath of God been manifested to men? *Answ.* These two waies.

1. By naturall light. 2. By the light of the word.

1. By the light of nature, or of conscience. There is such a power left in all mens hearts,(which is called conscience) that upon q sin commited,or good omitted summons men to the tribunall

of

of the supreme Majesty, telling them, that
they owe punishment to that soveraigne justice for
the commission of the one, and the omission of the
other. The Gentiles, who had nothing but the
light of nature, had this court of ᵗ judicature erected in them. *Rom.* 1. last. *Who knowing the judg-*
ment of God that they which commit such things are
worthy of Death &c. This was a principle rivetted,
and seated in all their hearts, this they knew full
well, they ᶠ acknowlegd it as true, (though they
were ignorant of, and denied many other truths)
that they which committed such, and such sinnes
were worthy of Gods *wrath:* for that is meant by
Death, that bearing the name of *death* here, which
is called *wrath* in the 18. verse. Hence it was
that many of the Heathens spake of a ᵗ golden eye,
a revengefull eye, an eye of justice that saw all,
and would be revenged for all the wickednesse,
that men committed.

This is farther set forth in that famous text; *Rom*
2. 15. where the apostle speaking of the Gentiles,
sayes, *their conscience also bearing witnesse, and*
their thoughts the meane while accusing, or els ex-
cusing one another. When they had sin'd their con-
sciences accused them, and told them, this they
ought not to have done, and there was one that
saw and would take vengeance for this: the ᵗ meaning is not (so much as the letter of the word
seems to import) as if so be the thoughts themselves did grate one upon another, one thought al-

Marginal notes:

ᵗ Δικασ'ειον συνειδ'ησεως appellat idem Hieroc.

ᶠ Επιγνόν]ες vid. Bez. in textum.

ᵗ Χρύσεον όμ-μα, ἔνδικον όμμα, δίκης ὀφθαλμὸς.

ᶠ Εςιν δικῆς ὀφθαλμὸς, ὃς τὰ παν'ϑ' ὁρᾷ κỳ Πέλας δὶ ἐςὶς ὁ Θε-ὸς ἐγγύθεν βλέπ]. ὁ μ Θεὸς (ὥσπὲρ δỳ κỳ ὁ πα-λαιὸς λό-γος) ἀρχλύ τὲ κỳ μέσα κỳ τελδοτλὼ ἔ-χον τῦ παν-τὸς, εὐθεία-περαίν] κ²πι φύσιν περιπο-ρδιομεν. τῦ δ' im'ϑ δίκη τῆς λειπομένων λειπομένων τιμωρὸς τῦ Θείε νόμε. *Plut. adv. Col.*

t Neq; enim sensus esse videtur, cogitationes se mutuò, *i.e.* aliam aliam accusasse, aut
excusasse, sed inter se, & quasi alternatim, ac per vices eum in quo reperiebantur prout
nempe unus idemq; nunc bene, nunc male ageret operaq; virtutum ac vitiorum vices
quasdam inter se obtinerent, similiter cogitationes inter se vices nunc excusandi nunc
accusandi habuisse. *Ladov. de Dieu.*

lowing

lowing it felf when it was good, and condemning it felf when it was evill, but the plainer fenfe feems to be; that they had accufing thoughts when they did evill, and excufing thoughts when they did well; the *man*, or *perfon* acquitting, or accufing himfelfe in his own thoughts according to the difference of his actions, his own *thoughts* (which is no more then the exercife of confcience) juftifying him when he did well, and condemning him when he did otherwife.

Moft men, if not all, efpecially when they fall into fome groffe fin, they have this warning, or remembrance from Confcience , thou haft finned, & thou wilt be damned for this another day. Now God by this meanes difcovers his hatred againft fin, and his wrath hanging over the finner. Confcience is Gods officer, it is his Herald to proclaime his wrath to men. If one Prince fend his Herald at armes to another Prince, or a Generall of an Army fends his challenge by drum or trumpet, there is then open warre, and all men know it. God hath fet up this light in men by which he proclaimes open warre to them in cafe they fin againft him. Wouldeft thou know whether God be angry yea or no ? look within, doeft thou feel no gripes, or prickings there? doth not thy heart fecretly fink and fall after fuch a fin? Oh miferable man what have I done! certainly I have brought my felf under the difpleafure of the Almighty. If thy confcience be not ftupid, or feared there are fuch fecret remembrances as thefe are: z And this is one way by which God inftructs the fons of men,

what

what the nature of fin is, and what they muſt expect, if ſo be they venture on it,

2. The ſecond way whereby the wrath of God
is manifeſted is, the light of the word. Now this is
twofold,

1. The light of the Law.
2. The light of the Goſpell.

1. It is manifeſted by the light of the Law, the
Law threatning nothing but death, curſes, plagues,
and vengeance to all fin, and ungodlineſſe
whatſoever: *Gen.* 2. 17. *In the day that thou eateſt*
thereof thou ſhalt ſurely dye. Curſed is every one that
continueth not in all things which are written in the
book of the Law to doe them. Gal. 3. 10. *wouldſt thou*
know whether the wrath of God hangs over men
by reaſon of fin, doe but read the 28. *Chap.* of *Deu-*
teron. There you ſhall find curſe upon curſe. In
the 15. verſe. *it is ſaid all theſe curſes ſhall come up-*
on thee, and overtake thee. Curſed ſhalt thou be in
the city, and curſed in the field, curſed ſhall be thy
basket , and curſed in thy ſtore, v. 20. *The Lord*
ſhall ſend upon thee curſing, vexation, & rebuke in all
that thou ſetteſt thine hand unto for to doe, untill thou
be deſtroyed, and untill thou periſh quickly, becauſe of
the wickedneſſe of thy doings, whereby thou haſt for-
ſaken me. The Law threatneth nothing but wrath.
it *worketh wrath. Rom.* 4. 15. It cauſes a ſenſe of
wrath, by threatning wrath to all the tranſgreſſors
of it.

2. Is it otherwiſe in the goſpell? no : the goſpel,
that reveals wrath too. The wrath of God *is revea*
led from heaven. As much as if the Apoſtle ſhould
say,

say: we the Apoſtles and Embaſſadours of God do
bring this meſſage from heaven, and publiſh it in
our goſpell to the world: that the wrath of God is
due to men by reaſon of ſin : all men by nature
are under wrath already, they are *children of wrath*
Eph. 2. and there is a day which is comming, when
this wrath ſhall come upon them to the utmoſt, if
they doe not believe, and repent.

Obj. Yea, but the goſpell reveales Chriſt, ſalvation, pardon of ſin?

An. True, this is the firſt intention of the
goſpell, and the firſt offer which it makes: but if
men *neglect ſo great ſalvation*, if they will not ſtoop
to goſpell tearms, and ſubmit to what it commands, if they will not *repent, and believe*, then
there is ſo much the more wrath, and the heavyer
vengeance *Heb*. 10. 28. 29. *He that deſpiſed Moſes*
Law, died without mercy, under two or three witneſſes.
Of how much ſorer puniſhment, ſuppoſe ye, ſhall he be
thought worthy, who hath troden under foot the ſonne
of God.

Beſides, the goſpell teacheth, that God will
judge the ſecrets of mens hearts. *Rom*. 2. 16. *In*
the day when God ſhall judge the hearts of men by
Jeſus Chriſt, according to my Goſpell. Thy ſecret
pride, covetouſneſſe, ambition, thy ſecret thefts,
adulteries, thy ſecret ſcorning of the word and ordinances; theſe muſt be all judged, the Goſpell that
hath ſaid ſo much in effect. It is according to the
Doctrine of the goſpell, that there muſt a generall
judgment paſſe on all a mans ſinnes, and therefore on the ſecrets of their hearts, his inward, and
most

Heb, 2. 3.

Mark 1. 14.
15.

moſt ſecret ſins. It is according to *my goſpell,* ſaith
the Apoſtle, that men muſt be judged:why, where
had *Paul ſaid ſo?* In that famous ſermon of his:
Acts: 17. 30.31. *And the times of this ignorance God
winked at, but now commandeth all men every where
to repent:becauſe he hath appointed a day in the which
he will judge the world in righteouſneſſe by that man
whom he hath ordained, whereof he hath given aſſu-
rance unto all men,in that he hath raiſed him frō the
Dead.* Or elſe he ſaies according to *his goſpell,* becauſe this was the tenor of the goſpell, a part and
portion of the goſpell, one of the moſt ordinary
and uſuall Doctrines therein revealed, he, and
the reſt of the Apoſtles going up and down, and
preaching the day of judgment unto men, bringing that as a maine argument why they ſhould repent,and believe; becauſe that there was a day a
comming, when they muſt be called to a reckon-
ing for all their ſinnes. So likewiſe it is the goſpell that ſaies 2. *Theſ.* 1. 7: 8.9. *The Lord Jeſus
ſhall be revealed from heaven,with his mighty Angels,
in flaming fire,takeing vengeauce on them that know
not God, and that obey not the goſpell of our Lord Jeſus Chriſt, who ſhall be puniſhed with everlaſting deſtruction from the preſence of the Lord, and from the
glory of his power.*

4. The fourth thing for the proſecution of the 4. Part.
Doctrine was, to make proof that this wrath of
God towards ſin,and ſinners hath been confirmed,
and made good by ſundry judgments inflicted upon ſinners from time to time. Now here we need
not ſtand long, the whole Book of God is full of
C cleare

cleare, and pregnant examplesto this purpose. You all know the story of the old world: it is said expresly, God brought *in the flood upon the world of the ungodly.* 2. *Peter.* 2. 5. You have all read, or heard the judgment that befell *Sodom, and Gomorrah*: It is recorded with a speciall note, *Gen.* 19 24. *Then the Lord rained upon Sodom, and Gomorrah brimstone, and fire from the Lord out of heaven.* The name of the Lord is used twice here, to shew, that it was a speciall hand from heaven that brought this. The Lord did this by himselfe, as it were: it was not a chance, or accident; (as some call the most fearfull judgments that ever have been executed) it was not the ill Crasis, and disposition of second causes, no, it was an immediate hand from heaven, it was Jehovah that did it.

We might instance in the examples of f *Pharaoh* and his Host, which were drowned in the red sea in the examples of g *Korah*, *Dathan*, *Abiram*, of h *Senacherib*, and diverse others.

From the old Testament we might passe to the New, and speak of the ends of *Judas*; *Ananias*, and *Sapphira*; *Herod.* These things you all know, much also might be fetched from Histories sacred, & prophane to confirme this. Ecclesiasticall Histories are full of examples in this kind. M. *Fox* in his Book of Martyrs hath a speciall tract to shew the fearfull ends of severall of the most Eminent persecutors of the Church, and people of God.

5. The Last thing for the clearing of the Doctrine is to shew the grounds, and reasons of this, why God takes this course many times in

this

e Hebraïsmus est, pluit Dominus a Domino de cœlo, pro Dominus pluit a se de cœlo. *Vatab.*
f Exod. 14.
g Numb. 16.
h Isai 37.
5 Partic.

this world to inflict upon notorious sinners some remarkable judgments:might it not be thought sufficient, that there are eternall punishments reserved for them?The reasons therefore why God doth this are these.

1. He doth it to put a stop to the Atheisme that is in the world. *The foole hath said in his heart there is no God. Pfal.*14.1.The Atheist sayes,we may doe as we list, the Lord sees not,neither doth he consider; good,and evill are all one to him, and he regards it not : or as they which are described in *Job. chap.* 21. *v.* 14. 15. *They say unto God, depart from us , for we desire not the knowledge of thy waies. what is the almighty that we should serve him? and what profit should we have if we pray unto him?*Now, when men are come to this passe , he will make them acknowledge him, whether they will or no. The Lord is marvelous patient,and long-suffering, he knowes how to right himselfe, and to be even with the sinner in the end: but if men will breake all bounds, if they will deny the majesty above, if they will scoff at his word, and make a mock of sin, if they will pluck up all religion by the very roots : he will not, he cannot any longer endure it , it stands him upon to keep up his authority in the world,he will be own'd,and acknowledged as God among his creatures. If nothing else will make the proud, & sturdy hearts of men to stoop, and yeeld to him, his Judgments shall *Pfal* 46. 10. *Be still, and know that I am God.* It is the voice of the Lord to the proud ones of the world. It seems they would not know that there was a God, or at

leaft

leaſt that the God of Iſrael was he, that was the true God; therefore was it that they were ſo mad againſt his people, *v.* 6. the *Heathen raged*: but, what is the next newes that we heare? *He uttered his voice; the earth melted.* As proud, and as ſtout as they are, no ſooner doth *He* ſpeak, but their ſpirits flag, & faint; thoſe great, and mighty ones who feared none , and car'd for none, they became as dead men: *he* uttered his voice, or as ſome read it he *gave his voice.* Who is this *He?* look back upon the former verſe, and you will quickly ſee, 'tis *God* that utters his voice. No ſooner doth God ſpeak a word , but their hearts faile them. Let *him* but ſhew himſelfe , of whom they made a mock but a little before, and queſtion'd whether there was any ſuch one, and then they feare, and tremble; they ſhrinke, and dare not hold up their heads. And why doth the Lord doe all this? Why doth he drive them to ſuch a ſtand? The end is ſet down at the 11. verſe. He will be known as God, amongſt the worſt of men. *Be ſtill, and know that I am God,* and then it followes, *I will be exalted among the heathen, I will be exalted in the earth.* That wicked Pharaoh, one of the worſt of me͂, who blaſphe͂ed againſt heave͂ & ſaid, *who is the Lord, that I ſhould obey his voice to let Iſrael goe? I know not the Lord, neither wil I let Iſrael goe. Exod.* 5. 2. This bold, this proud wretch, after he had ſeene the hand of the Lord lifted up, and felt his plagues, he is forced to know who the Lord was , and to let Iſrael goe.

2 Reaſon. 2. The Lord doth this to render men inexcuſable

fable. *Rom.* 2. 1. Therefore thou art *inexcufable*
0 man, whofoever thou art that judgeft. Judgeft, how
is that? that judgeft men worthy of death by fin:
that was Gods verdict, and fentence touching finners, and this all men knew by the light of nature
and had thefame judã:ment , and apprehention'
of it in themfeves: as it is c. 1. v. 32 when as
a man knowes by the light, and checks of his own
confcience , that the wrath of God is due unto
him by reafon of fin, when he fees all the curfes
that are revealed in the Law, and the fearfull vengeance denounced in the gofpell againft all unbe-
lieving, and unrepenting finners, this makes him
greatly inexcufable : but when he fhall fee the
judgments of God executed before his eyes, and
many of the fame ranck, and kind of finners ftruck
dead in the midft of their abominations, if yet he
goe on in the fame fins, this makes him beyond
meafure inexcufable. If a man fhould fee an hundred theeves, or robbers hung up one after another
at feverall affifes, and yet after this, this man himfelfe fhould play the theefe, who would pity that
man if he came to the fame end? he knowes thee-
very to be an unwarrantable, & dangerous thing,
the law is againft it, and many have been punifhed
for it from time to time before his eyes, this makes
him inexcufable : fo it is in this cafe: If God take
other men in the midft of their fins, if he take them
in the midft of their drinking, quaffing, and ca-
roufing, as he did Belfhazzar in the midft of his
cups, or ftrike them with fome fecret, and fudden
blow in the midft of their chambering and wan-

C 3   tonefle

toneſſe, as he did the young man in the proverbs, who when he went to the harlots houſe, *had a dart ſtruck through his liver.* Chap. 7. 23. or by an immediate hand from heaven, and an Angell ſent to that purpoſe, ſhall puniſh them in the midſt of their pride, tyranny, and perſecution, as he dealt with Herod. If after all this, when a man hath ſeen ſuch cleare, and manifeſt Judgments from heaven, on the perſons of others, he ſhall live in the ſame, or worſe ſins ; if he ſhall continue a drunkard, an adulterer, a perſecutor, and oppoſer of the ſaints, and of religion after all this, who can ſay this man is not juſtly puniſhed? The word is plaine, and expreſſe againſt ſuch, and ſuch ſinnes; the end and iſſue of them is there revealed, and the judgments of God have ratifyed it, and con-firmed it; this man is left without all excuſe. *Now God will have every mouth to be ſtopped; and all the world become guilty before God. Rom. 3. 19.*

Reaſ. 3 .

3. The Lord inflicts judgments upon ſome, that they might be for examples unto others. 2. Peter. 2. 6. *Turning the citties of ſodom, and Gomor-rah into aſhes, condemning them with an overthrow, makeing them an enſample unto thoſe that after ſhould live ungodly.* Here is both the judgment, and the reaſon of it expreſſed. *He turned them into aſhes, and he condemned them with an overthrow*: he had condemned their wickedneſſe before in his owne

Καταςροφὴ τέλος. ἐρή- μωσις Phav

thoughts, and adjudg'd them worthy of ſome ſe-vere plague, and that plague muſt be nothing leſſe then a totall deſtruction, a totall overthrow; he would ſo deſtroy them as to make an utter end

of

of them : for that is the meaning of the word. And why would he do so?it was to *make thē an example;* he set them up as an example, he had prepar'd thē for an example in his own thoughts before, he had fitted, and defigned them for it; now this is the edition, and fetting forth as it were,of what he had fram'd, and contriv'd before. *Saint Peter* had men-tioned two great editions of the wrath of God be-fore, one was in the Angels that fell: He caft *them down to hell,* v. 4. Here was wrath indeed. Ano-ther was in the old world. He brought in the floud upon a whole world. v. 5. here was the fecond great edition of his wrath , if I may fo fpeak. And the third was in that of *Sodom,*and *Gommorah,*thefe he 1 conftituted,& framed for *an *example,*that is, for a figne,a token,a fure, a ftanding remembrance * of what he meant to doe with others in the like kind: *And therefore is it faid, unto thofe that* m *after fhould live ungodly.* If any had a mind after this to play the Atheifts,to caft off all the thoughts of God, of religion, and to riot it in their lufts, as the *Sodo-mites,* they might here fee as in a map, what their doome was like to bee. S. *Paul* reckons up a whole Catalogue of Judgments which befell the Ifrae-lites. 1.*Cor.*10.11.It is faid,*now all thefe things hap-pened to them for enfamples.* the meaning is not that thofe Judgments came by chance upon them for how could they then be intended as examples, as he faies they were. Neither doth he fay *divifim,* and a part, that thefe things *happened* , and were *examples* , but he fpeaks *conjunctim,*knit-ting them up both in one fentence, they happened

as

1 Τεʃεικὸς conftituit. *Seq.* poneus *Vulg:*

* Υπόδειγμα σημεῖον. Hefych.

m Τῶν μελ-λόντων ἀσε-βεῖν.ἀσεβὴς δίοντὲς ὁ μὴ σεβόμενΘ τ Θεὸν. Ph. ἀσεβὴς. ἀ-σεΘ. ἁμαρ-τωλὸς Hef.

as examples, or for examples, that is, those things which corrupt, and carnall hearts look upon as chances, and misfortunes, he in the course of his providence orders that they should come to passe, that they might be examples , therefore in the 6. verse it is said , these things were our ex-

* ἐγενήθησαν amples , or they were * made our examples, being ordained, and appointed of him so to be.

n Τύπος. *Examples*] that is patterns, samplers, and simili-
τύπον δὲ ἕξι tudes, of what he intended to doe in after times.
πεοςδοκωμέ- These were some of the first draughts, and cop-
νη δήλωσις pies of his judgments, that men might see, as he
διὰ μιμήσε- had begun, so he intended to goe on, and there-
ως δεικτι- fore they are said to be examples, *written for in-*
κῶς τὸ μέλ- *struction, or admonition. Examples* they were so in
λον ὑπομαι- their primitive intendment: and they are *written*
νον. Phav. too, left upon record, that *we* might take warning by them *on whom the ends of the world are come.* The last age of this world is like to be the worst, and therefore is it said, *in the last dayes perilous*

ο Νυθεσίαν *times shall come* , for there shall be sinners of such
Admonitio- and such a sort, 2. *Tim.* 3. 1. Now God hath pro-
nē: pretiosum vided for this before hand, he hath given many
vccabulum, noteable examples of his judgments in former a-
quo significa- ges, which men, if they were wise, would hide in
catur rectis their hearts, and keep ever by them; and that was
monitis mens his end in makeing such examples, that they might
quasi prius be for *admonition:* o a pretious word (as one calls
emota suo it) signifying the bringing of the mind back to it
loco restitui, selfe againe by some wholesome rebuke or other,
vel antea that was formerly out of its place; or els it signifi-
fluctuans eth the setling of the mind, that before was fluctu-
componi. ating
Bez. in
1.Cor. 10

ating, and wavering. All men are apt to think fleightly of fin, they look upon fin, as a harmleffe thing, that hath no venome, nor fting in it, they play and dally with it, as little children would do with a Snake. All this while the underftanding is a fleep, the mind is out of its place, it judges not of things according to the nature of them. But when the Lord from heaven beginnes to fhoot his arrowes, when they fee men taken in the midft of their impieties, and punifhed with fome grievous, and fearfull judgments, then the mind beginnes to be awakened, and a mans thoughts begin to recollect themfelves, certainly fin is not fuch a trifle, it is not a toy, an empty notion, as the moft of men doe make it. Thefe are the warnings of God to men : his judgments executed in the world, are as fo many monûents, ftanding remembrances of his difpleafure againft fin. This is the laft reafon of the point.

The Application followes.

The firft vfe may be a word of Terror, & it is able to fhake the heart of every unrepentant finner under heaven. Is there fuch wrath in God as hath been opened? hath it been all along manifefted and revealed? have his judgments confirmed it ? this may ftrike a dampe, a terror on the heart of every wretched, unrepenting finner in the world. Here thou mayeft fee what thy cafe is, and what thy doome will certainly bee: the wrath of the great God, the God of heaven, and earth is kindled againft thee, it burneth, and waxes hot againft thee, yea it will one day confume thee, and deftroy thee:

D   it

it will tumble thee down into endlesse, easelesse,&
remedilesse torments. This were enough to shake
the proudest Nimrods of the world, and to make
the most stout hearted sinner tremble like an *aspen
leafe*, would he but consider it. The case is plaine,
and cleare: the judgment sure and certaine.

The wrath of God is revealed from heaven, its a
plaine, a manifest thing, its written with a sun-
beame, and there needs be no question of it, thine
owne conscience, that araignes, accuses, and con-
demnes thee: its the voice and cry of conscience,
if thou lyest in such, and such abominations, thou
must be damned, the word sayes it, the Law hath
pronounced it a thousand times over and over,
the gospell that ratifyes, and confirmes it, and the
judgments of God executed in the world, they
put it out of doubt.

Oh miserable man or woman, who ever thou
bee, be thou young or old, rich or poore, be thy
rank or condition whatsoever it be, that lyest in thy secret thefts, adulteries, oaths, propha-
nations of the sabbath, whose heart riseth at God,
and his waies, that lovest thy ignorance, wordli-
nesse, or what ever sin it bee, that I cannot name
in which thou livest, and art resolved so to doe!
Oh miserable, forlorne creature! The God of heaven and earth is set against thee, the God of heaven,& earth is resolved to plague &punish thee.

Art thou able to dwell with everlasting burnings, or to stand before a devouring fire? Art
thou a fit match for the Almighty? canst thou grap-
ple with thy maker? art thou strong enough to o-
vercome

vercome his Almightyneffe? What is become of
all the mighty finners in the world? what is become of the world of the ungodly? Were they
not all fwallowed up together, and devoured as
in a moment? What is become of the wicked So-
domites? Were they not confumed with fire and
brim-ftone? Nay, thats not all, they *fuffer the
vengeance of eternall fire,* they lye flaming in the
fire of hell, and are fcorched with the wrath of   Jude 5.7.
God there for ever. What is become of *Cain,* and
Judas, and all the rabble of the ungodly? Hath
not this wrath of the Lord lighted on them, and
are they not for ever miferable; this is thy doome
& portion alfo, who continueft in thine abomina-
tions. *Tophet is ordained of old : yea, for the King*   Ifai. 30. 33.
it is prepared, he hath made it deep, and large : the
the pile thereof is fire, and much wood; the breath of
the Lord, like a ftreame of brimftone, doth kindle it:
There is elbow roome enough in hell for all the
drunkards, fwearers, Atheifts in the world. *He*
hath made it deepe, and large, it will hold them all,
there is no feare of it: this is the place prepared for
thee. Be thou a great finner, or little finner, it matters not, if fo be thou be an unrepenting finner, it
may be thy fin is foe fecret way of ū juft gain, it may
be it is wilfull ignorance, conftant negleft of holy
duties, be it what it will be, if thou be an unrepentant finner, if thou keep thy fin in thy bofome, if
thou hide it as a fweet morfell under thy tongue,
the wrath of the Lord is gone out againft thee.
Oh how great, how dreadfull is that wrath? *Jerem.*
10. v. 10. *The Lord is the true God, he is the liveing*

D 2   *God*

God, and an everlasting King: at his wrath the earth shall tremble: and the nations shall not be able to abide his indignation. Revel. 6. 14, 15, 16, 17. And the heaven departed as a scrole, when it is rolled together, & every mountain & Island were moved out of their places: And the Kings of the earth, and the great men, & the rich mē, & the chiefe captaines, & the mighty men, and every bond-man, and every free-man hid themselves in the dens, and in the rocks of the mountaines, And said to the mountaines, and rocks fall on us, and hide us from the face of him that sitteth on the throne, and from the wrath of the Lamb: For the great day of his wrath is come, and who shall be able to stand?

Thou mayest mock at the word now, and despise the messengers of the Lord, and make a light matter of sin, hell, wrath, and judgment, and every such thing. Yea but then shalt thou cry to the rocks, & mountaines to fall on thee, & to shelter thee from the wrath of the Lord, and the fiercenesse of his anger. *The wrath of the King is as the roaring of a Lyon,* but what is the wrath of the King of Kings, and Lord of Lords? when the Almighty shall strech forth his owne hand against a poore rebellious creature, one that had wallowed in his filthinesse, and took his swinge in his base, and swinish lusts, and he shall set his owne almightynesse on worke to make him miserable, Oh how great must that misery bee! *Revelation* 1. 7. *Behold He commeth, and every eye shall see him,* all kindreds of the earth shal wail because of *him.* There is a mighty emphasis lies on it, it is *he* that com-

meth

meth, who is that? look back at the 5. verſe, and
you will ſee it is *Jeſus Chriſt, the faithfull witneſſe,
the firſt begotten of the dead, the prince of the
Kings of the earth,* unto whom *glory, and dominion*
is due for ever and ever. *Behold he* commeth it is
uſhered in with a note of aſtoniſhment and a-
mazement: it is not a poore deſpiſed Chriſt, it is
not a carpenters ſonne that now appeares, he commeth not in that meane, low, & abjeƈt way as once
he did; no, it is the glorious Lord Jeſus, it is the
the faithfull witneſſe, one that hath received publique teſtimony in heaven of his truth and faithfullneſſe in his fathers worke, it is he that was raiſed up by the glory of the Father, whom he hath
ſet at his owne right hand, *Far above all principality
and powers, and might and dominion, and every name
that is named, not only in this world, but alſo in that
which is to come.* 'Tis he commeth, he comes not
in a poore meane and abjeƈt manner, no he commeth with clouds, he ſhall come *in the glory of his
father,* and all *the holy Angells with him. Behold he
commeth.* Or elſe we may refer this to the follow-
ing verſe. v. 8. I am Alpha and Omega, the beginning & the ending ſaith the Lord, which is, &
which was, & which is to come; the Almighty. It is
that Eternall, that Almighty one. Behold he come-
eth. So in the Epiſtle of Jude v. 14. *Behold the Lord
commeth.* Here we have a *behold* too. *The Lord
commeth with ten-thouſands of his Saints.* To ſee
ten thouſand Saints, and thouſand thouſandes
of Angells comming to Judgment, Oh what a
dreadfull ſight would this bee! but it is the Lord

that

that commeth in the front, and head of thefe, they are but his followers & attendants. The *Lord*] he whom thou haft hated, fcorned, oppofed all this while, it is the Lord that cōmeth whofe cōmands thou haft made bold withall , and regarded no more: then the duft under thy feet. The Lord commeth to *execute vengeance v.* 15; who faid ex. preffely thou fhouldft not be drunken, riotous, un- juft, abufe his mercies and the like: this glorious mighty Lord, he himfelfe commeth, he whom thou haft difhonoured, provoked, blafphemed fo ma- ny yeares together, and yet he let thee alone, but now thou fhalt pay for all, he comes to *execute judgement upon all, and to convince all that are un- godly amongft them* , he will fpare none, high nor low, rich nor poore, all fhall ftand before the judgement feat. But is that all, it followes, *he will convince them of all their ungodly deeds, which they have ungodly committed.* Thou canft be tipfy in a corner, and commit filthineffe in fecret, and re- ferve fome hidden clofe haunts of fin which are remote from the eyes of men, but thou fhalt not carry it fo, *the Lord will convince all that are ungod- ly among them* , as fubtill, and as cunning an hy- pocrite as thou art, thou fhalt be unmafked, the Lord will lay thee open before men, and Angells, thy bafeneffe, and underhand dealing, thy dodg- ing, and dawbing in matters of religion fhall be brought to light at that day. Thou fayeft as thofe mockers did, wher is the promife of his comming? What is this day of Judgment, hell, and wrath that Minifters tell us fo much off? Tufh thefe are but

Bug-

Bug-beares to fright little children with; and Prea-
chers are grown so proud now a daies as they will
have all men come to their bowes, and have an
awe, and reverence of them: but let us not be so
weak to hearken to such tales. But what followeth? He will convince them *of all their hard spee-*
ches which ungodly sinners have spoken against him.
Alas! for thee poore man. It is not the Minister
thou speakest against, those thy wicked, thy accursed, thy hard speeches, they are *against him.* The
Lord will not be mocked, neither will he suffer
his creatures to laugh him to scorne. He will convince thee one day, that sin, hell, and wrath are
not dreames, fancies, and idle tales, & when thou
hast lyen some millions of yeares in those insuffe-
rable torments, and hast *eternity, for ever lying*
before thee to think what thou hast still to endure,
then thou wilt see, whether sin be sin, yea, or no,
whether the wrath of God be a rediculous thing
yea or no. Oh feare and tremble at the thoughts
of these things: that which hath been said might
make the heart of every unrepentant sinner
shake, and his joynts to tremble. This is the
first use.

The second use, and all the use in the generall, Use 2.
that shall be made of the point in hand, is an exhortation to Repentance: Is the wrath of God
gone out against all the ungodlinesse and unrighteousnesse of men? Oh Repent, Repent betimes,
ere this wrath come upon you. I have lately exhorted you to repentance, by the mercies of God,
by his love and goodnesse, and the sweet provisi-
on

on that he hath made, he hath raiſed up his ſon the
Lord Jeſus to give that bleſſing to you. You need
not ſay the work is too hard, it is a thing im-
poſſible for us to repent. You have heard where
your ſtrength lies: I muſt now goe another way to
worke, and exhort you to repentance by the
Judgments of the Lord, the text which I am hand-
ling calls for it, and the providences of the Lord,
they call for it alſo. *Knowing the terror of the Lord
we perſwade men,* ſaith the Apoſtle: ſo muſt we do
likewiſe. Let me ſpeak to every ſoul of you that
belongs to this place, be thy rank, or condition
whatſoever it bee, be thou in higher or meaner
place, Repent, and that ſpeedily before the indignation of the Lord come upon you to the uttermoſt. I remember what John Baptiſt ſaid to the
Phariſees, and Sadduces that came to his baptiſme:
it may bee looked upon as a kind of argument to
preſſe the doctrine of repentance more cloſely on
them, *Math. 3. 7. who hath warned you to flee from
the wrath to come.* I may ſay concerning you of this
place, the wrath of God is already come, it hath
already appeared, it is revealed from heaven in
the face of the open ſun, that all that paſſe by you
cannot but take notice of it. Oh repent, repent,
left this wrath come upon you to the uttermoſt.
Luke 13:4. 5 *Suppoſe yee thoſe eighteene upon whom
the tower in Siloam fell & ſlew them, thinke yee
that they were ſinners above all men that dwell
in Jeruſalem, I tell you nay: but except ye repent, ye
ſhall all likewiſe periſh.* He doth not ſay that they
which ſuffered thoſe things were no ſinners at all,

or

or that they were little sinners, but he would not have them that escaped *that* danger put off the busineſſe from themſelves, as if ſo be they that were ſlaine, and made the immediate examples of Gods diſpleaſure were the onely ſinners in Jeruſalem : no, he tels *them, their* ſins might be as great as any of the reſt; and therefore he adviſes them to look about themſelves, for unleſſe they repented, they likewiſe ſhould periſh. Do not thinke my bretheren, that the poore children that were cruſhed to death, the men and women that had their armes and legs broken, or diſioynted, their bodyes ſorely bruiſed were ſinners above all the people in *Witney*, or that there are no other ſinners but the amongſt you. Nay I tell you all, except yee repent, ye ſhall all likewiſe periſh. Vnleſſe thou, ô man, or woman, who ever thou art, repent of thy drunkenneſſe, lying, covetuouſneſſe, of thy coldneſſe and indifferency in religion thou ſhalt one day periſh, the word ſaies it, conſcience tels thee ſo, the damned in Hell they feele it to be ſo.

Oh what a ſtrange paſſe are men come unto the wrath of God is revealed from heaven, and yet they will not believe. God hath teſtifyed it from heaven, that every drunkard, and ſwearer, and prophane perſon ſhall certainly be damned; and yet men will not believe. 1. *Cor.* 6. 9. *Know ye not that the unrighteous*, &c. why, This is a plaine thing, an evident, a manifeſt thing, a man may ſay it is dark at noone day, if he will, but this is cleare and beyond all doubt it ſelfe. *Know ye not that the un-*

E
righteous

righteous ſhall not inherit the Kingdome of God. The gate of heaven ſhall never be opened to any unrighteous ſoule, no uncleane thing ſhall ever enter there. No, if the holy, and righteous God be in heaven, thou which art an unholy and an unrighteous ſoul ſhalt never get there; and if the Saints and Angells ſtay in heaven, thou which art ſo unlike them ſhalt never come there. Oh think on this for the Lords ſake. *From heaven* thou art pointed out to deſtruction, all the *leaves* in the Bible make againſt thee, all the Judgments that ever God hath executed are cleare and plaine before thine eyes; and yet men will not believe! What will become of this Atheiſticall generation? There is no man feares, there is no man conſiders his way. Though the bleſſed God from heaven tell men that their ungodlineſſe & unrighteouſnes doth bring his wrath upon them, & wil damne the in the end, they wil not believe it, they will not lay it to heart. The word that threatneth wrath, the Judgméts of God, they reveale & make known this wrath, the devils in hell they believe & tremble at it, & the damn'd, they feel it, & yet the ſtout hearted ſonnes of men they care not for it. 1. *Cor.* 10.

p Παραζη-
λῶν, παρο-
ξυνων, παρο-
ξυνων. *Pha.*
q Παραζη-
λῶν περ-
ξυνων, πα-
ρεξιῶν. *He-*
ſjeb.

22. *Do we provoke the Lord to jealouſy, are we ſtron-ger then he?* Do we incenſe, p exaſperate, and put the Lord himſelfe to it to ſhew what he can do? are we content the Lord ſhould doe his worſt? doe we q equall and compare our ſelves with him? dare we juſtle, and contend with him for maſtery? Oh fearefulll are you come to this point? let the Lord do his worſt, we ſhall deale with him

and

and his wrath well enough. Oh desperate forlorn
man! *It is a fearfull thing to fall into the hands of
the living God.* Oh repent, repent. It was one of ^{Heb. 10.1.} the dying words of a famous Martyr. Repent O
England, repent, repent, so say I to you, *O Witney,*
repent, repent, otherwise I feare some more
dreadfull plagues will befall you. You that have
ungodly neighbours, servants, or friends go to thē
& ask them, what meane you to lie in your ignorance, prophaneneffe, neglect of God and holy
things still? What do you love to be damned? and
are you well pleased to be fent packing to hell as
foone as you dye? For the Lords fake fet upon
this work fpeedily, if you do not I feare fome worfe
thing will come next. Certainely, my Brethren, the
hand of the Lord is gone out againft you in this
late Tragedy; (for fo it fhould be called it was
not a Comedy, no, no, it was a Tragedy, a dolefull Play, it had a dolefull end, a bloudy, a fad end.
Thofe of you that heard the fcreekings and bitter
complaints, the fearfull heart-piercing cries, that
faw the broken bones, the difioynted armes, the
dead carcaffes of fo many children, will fay it was
a Tragedy indeed, a dolefull play) and the wrath
of God hath been revealed from heaven, it is revealed from heaven againft thee O *Witny.* If there
be any mockers or fcoffers in the congregatiō that
are come to deride the word, I fay if there be any
fuch, though I hope better things of the moft of
you, yet if there be any fecret fcoffer in a corner,
I fhall fay to him as Job did to his friends, when

they

they had made light of his calamity, and said, it was juft. *Job.* 11. 3. *Suffer me that I may speake, and after that I have spoken, mock on.* You that make fo light of the hand of God,& laugh atall his judgemēts,heare themeſſage which the Lord hath fent, & if after that ye have a mind to mock,then mock ye on, take your fill of laughter, and it may be you may have your belly full of mocking another day.

Brethren, miſtake me not, my aime is not to make you fad, (though it is fit,indeed,you ſhould be humbled for your ſins.) Alas, what pleaſure can it be to the poor ſervants, and meſſengers of the Lord to make any one fad ? No, no, it is your good, and happineſſe, it is the welfare and happineſſe of this place I aime at, and I hope by that time you have heard all I have to fay,you will be convinced, that it is fo indeed. Let me ſpeak to you as the Apoſtle doth to his Corinthians. 2.*Cor.* 11. 1. *Would to God you could bare with me a little in my folly, and indeed beare with me.* And then at the 20 verſe. *for ye ſuffer,if a man bring you into bondage, if a man devoure you, if a man take of you, if a man exalt himſclfe, if a man ſmite you on the face.* Many, I feare, are apt to plead for their luſts and corruptions, for their games and ſports, which have devoured them, and conſumed them, and brought them low, and is there not as much reaſon they ſhould beare with the word which comes in all plainneſſe, and faithfulneſſe to doe them good ? Certainly my brethren the hand of

the

the Lord is lifted up, the great and dreadfull God, the King of the whole earth hath shewen himselfe in the midst of you. I could have hoped there would not be found a man in this place, that was come to that height of Atheisme, as to say, this was not the hand of God, this was not a judgement, it was only a chance, a mis-fortune, & such a thinge might fall out, the house was weak, the beam was not strong enough to support such a multitude. I could here cease speaking to such a man, and desire a corner to turne aside & weep in, & even power out rivers of teares in his behalf. It was that wch made the Prophet cry out in the like case. *Isai.* 26. 11. *Lord, when thy hand is lifted up, they will not see.* How was the Lords hand lifted up? Do but read the former verses and you will find, in the 9. verse we heare of his judgements being abroad, and in the 10. verse, we heare of favour shewen to the wicked. *Let favour be shewen to the wicked, yet will he not learne righteousnesse.* The Lords hand was lifted up in a way of judgment, and in a way of mercy, it was his righteous judgment that some were cut off, and it was his mercy that others were spared, and yet when his hand was lifted up so Emenently, they would not see. The Lord hath shewen both his severity, and his goodnesse amongst you, severity to them that sufferred, and goodnesse to you that were preserved. Is it not the Lords goodnesse? or to returne to the Prophets expression, is it not a *favour* shewen to thee, that thou hast thy life given thee, when others were

crushed

cruſhed to death? is it not a favour that thou art
ſafe and ſound, when others had their limbes broken, their bodies grievouſly bruiſed? Oh this was
that which ſo moved the Prophet, or the church
her ſelfe that is brought in ſpeaking in that chapt.
that ſhe knew not well how to beare it. *Lord when
thy hand is lifted up they will not ſee.* It is a pathe-
ticall ſpeech, and it ſavours of ſomewhat a grie-
ved and troubled ſpirit. Oh the hard-hearted-
neſſe, the pride and ſtoutneſſe that is in men,
not to ſee when the Lords hand is ſo lifted up.
What is thy heart flint, and thy Bowels made of
braſſe? will not wrath from heaven, great wrath
affect thee? Read what followes in the ſame verſe.
They will not ſee , but they ſhall ſee. Thou winkeſt
with thine eyes now, but the Lord will open them
at laſt, thou wilt not believe this is the wrath of
God, thou wilt believe it to purpoſe another day,
and it may be that day is not far off. That I may
ſhew you the wretchedneſſe of this diſpoſition,
not to ſee and acknowledge the Lord in ſuch great
things, but to lay them upon chance, misfortune,
ſecond cauſes, and the like. Conſider, 1 This is
a meer heatheniſh temper, the Heathens could not
do worſe then ſo , the Philiſtines they ſaid if the
matter fell not out ſo and ſo, as they had caſt it,
it was not the hand of the Lord that ſmote them,
but it was a chance that happened. 1. *Sam.* 6. 9. ſhall
we make our ſelves Philiſtines? ſhall we compare
our ſelves with the worſt of the heathens ? Nay,
ſome of the heathens have acknowledged the
Pro-

ᵣProvidence of God in ſuch ꜰmatters,ₜ they lookt
upon evills befalling them as the juſt puniſhments
of their ſinnes, they have feared and trembled
at the things that have come to paſſe , as ac-
knowledging a Divine Power that was the
cauſe of them.

ʳ *Vide Lip-
ſiumPhyſio-
log. Stoic.
l.1.Diſſert.
undecimâ et
ſeq. Arrian.
lib.1.cap.
6.& 12ᵐᵒ*

Jamblich. de vitâ Pythag. cap. 28. Stobæum Eclog. Phyſic. lib. 1. cap. 3.

ˢ Κεφάλαιον δὲ τῆς εἰρημένων, ὅτι ὁ θεὸς νομοθέτης ἂν ἅμα κ̀ δίκασὸς, τί δὲ ἢ
μ̈ τὰ ἀγαθὰ, ἀναιρεῖ δὲ τὰ κακά. Διὸ κ̀ πάντη κακῶν ὅ̓τιν ἀναιτ^Θ. κ̀ δ'
κακωθέντας αὐτεξυσίαις ὁρμαῖς, κ̀ τ̀ ἐν αὐτοῖς ὀρθὸν λόγον ἀμνημονήσαντας,
ὡς μ̈ κακὺς κολάζει χτι τ̀ νόμον ἀπαγορεύοντα τὰ κακὰ, ὡς δὲ ἀνθρώπες τῇ
ἐπεισιόσῃ ὅ̓ιπλοκῇ τῇ νόμῳ πρὸς τίω προαίρεσιν, ἢ δὴ τύχίω καλῦμεν. εἰ γὰ
ἁπλῶς τ̀ ἄνθρωπον, ἢ ἀνθρωπ^Θ, κολάζει ὁ νόμ^Θ, ἀλλ' ἢ κακὸς. Hierocl. in
aur. carm. paulo poſt. Ὁυ γὸ ὡς ἔτυχε τὰ ἀλγεινὰ τῖς ἀνθρώποις δαίμω ἢ ;
ἅπερ θεὸς, κ̀ δίκης ὄεςι προεστήκασιν ἡμῶν, τίω ἀξίαν μοιρὰν ἐφ' ἑκάστοις ἱπέ-
μπτες. ᵗ Nec Homerus hoc neſcivit: qui de Græcis adflictis cauſam reddit.
—— ἐπεὶ ὔτε νοήμονες ὔτε δίκαιοι.
Πάντες ἔσαν. Lipſ. diſſ. 16. Δίκα·τοὶ δίκα χρόνι^Θ. ἀλλ' ὅμῶς ἴσω τι σευ'
ἔλαθεν ὅταν ἔχῃ τιν' ἀσεβῆ βρoτῶν τὸ τοι κακὸν σοδῶκις ἔχ̥ἐ βρoτοῖς ἀεὶ
γὸ εὐπήρ]κσιν οἱ διὸς κύβοι. Εurip. apud Stobæum in Phyſ. ᵘ Ἡ γὸ ἡμετέρα
κακία, κ̀ κείσις θεία, τιμωρεμένη τίω πονηείαν, τὰ χαλεπὰ συμφόρησι.Hieroc.
in Aur. Car.

The ₓ Roman Emperours, yea thoſe among them
who have been moſt ᵧ prophane & wicked, and
at ſometimes have contemned God, religion it
ſelfe, and have lookt the judgments of God in the
face, with pride,& ſcorne,at other times they have
been ſurprized with a Panick feare. If they heard

ˣ *Circa reli-
giones talem
accepimus.
Tonitrua &
fulgura pau-
lò infirmius
expaveſcebat
Suet. in Au-
guſto.*

ᵧ Auſus interdum non ſolum vultum attollere: ſed etiam τ̀ βρονταῖς ἐκ μηχανῆς
τινος ἀν]ιβροντᾶν, κ̀ τ̀ ἀστραπαῖς ἀνταστράπ]ξιν, κ̀ ὁπότε κεραυνὸς καταπέσοι,
λίθον ἀνταχοντίζειν Refert. Caſaub. de Caligula ex Dione.

but

z Nam qui
Deos tanto-
pere con-
temneret,ad
minima to-
nitrua & ful-
gura conni-
vere, caput
obvolvere,
advero ma-
jora prori-
pere se è stra-
to, sub lect-
uq; condere
solebat .
Sue:Calig.

a Moris fuit
cùm tonaret
aut fulgeret,
aut terra mo
veret, con-
tinuò pro
mutua salute
diis vota fun-
dere Caussab.
ex Philostra:o
Cujus verba
.apponit

but z thundering, & lightning, they would croutch under their bedds, and hide their heads, fearing that some plague from heaven was comming upon them. The Historian reports of *Caligula*, that wicked Emperour, that he which did so much des. pise the Gods, upon the least crack of thunder, or flash of lightning was wont to wink , & to wrap up his head; and if the thunder, and lightening were a little greater then ordinary, he would get off the bed on which he lay, and hide himself under the bed. Yea, it was a a Custome among some of the Heathens, when there was thunder, or lightening, or an earth-quake to pray to their Dietyes for on anothers safety and preservation. Nay, the very devills in hell *believe, and tremble,* the scripture saies it, and it is so: they have seen all the judgments that have been already executed, they know them to be his judgments, and tremble at them. They know all the threatnings of the word to be true; and beleeve they shall be accomplished. They know that the day of judgment will come, they look for it, and tremble at the thoughts of it. What art thou worse then the wickedest heathen that ever was? then the blackest Fiend in hell ? Oh wretched creature! Pluck off the vizard, shew what thou art. Do not defile, & abuse that pretious name of Christian: thou a Christian, and worse then a Heathen, worse then the very devills in hell?

2. Not to acknowledge God in such terrible astonishing things as these are, it is the flattest most down right Atheisme that ever was. It is to deny

God

God himfelfe, that there is fuch a Majefty as the
Majefty of heaven and earth, it is to deny the
word, it is to deny all his judgments, it is in effect
to call all the great workes of God that ever he
hath wrought in the world meer accidents, and
chances; it is to make the floud a meer chance,
it is to make the burning of *Sodom*, and *Gomorah*
a meer chance, in a word it is to make every thing
that is recorded in fcripture as a punifhment of fin
and finners meer cafualities and chances. Oh monftrous, abominable blafphemy ! was there ever
greater blafphemy then this? This is to deny God,
to deny his word, to become a ftark downright
k Atheift. Doeft thou believe there are any fuch
things as judgments: certainly if there be this was
one. What is a judgment, but onely a punifhment
laid on men for fin, and that which makes it more
remarkeably a judgment is, when men are taken
in the midft of their fins. Now that ftage-plaies,
are fins, fearfull and abominable fins, both in them
that act them, and them that behold them, we
need not labour much to proove.

1. We might urge, where doth the word of God
tolerate fuch Paf-times? the word fayes we fhould
redeeme the time, be fwift to fpeak, watch unto pray-
er. If thou canft not afford one houre to heare a
Sermon, to pray, to performe religious dueties in,
doth the word afford thee, three, foure houres, or
whole nights to fit up at a play?

2. But this is leaft of all; ftage-playes are ab-
folutely againft the word, the word forbids idle
words, foolifh words, jefting, it forbids unchaft

F   lookes

k Τὸ π̃   Å
ταῦτον δὲ̀
(repete ex
fuperioribus
ἐὰν ἀπεγνὸ-
ητον π̃ π̃ν,
ἡ κακῶς
φεντηζόμε-
νον ὁπιϑό-
μεν) τὸ μὴ
ὁιεϑη ἐῖναι-
ϑεον, ἡ ὅτπα
μὴ αεγνοῦϰ-
ἡ αεγνοῦντα
μὴ ἀγαϑὸν
ᾗ ἡ δηϊς-
ον. Hier.

Τολμῶ κ̃-
τειϑεῖρ μὴ
τοῖ᾽ ἐκ ἐϊϛ
ϑεὸς; κακῶν
ἢ ἐυψυχῶ-
νς ἐκπλὴτ-
τϛοί μϛ.

Tragicus
quidam apud
Lypf.

Eph. 5.16.
James 1.19.
1 Pet. 4.7.

lookes, unchaft apparrell, unchaft gestures, every thing that might be an occasion of sin : the Scripture faith, *Whosoever looketh upon a woman to lust after her, hath committed adultery with her already in his heart.* Againe it sayes *The light of the body is the eye, if thine eye be evill thy whole body is full of darknesse:* stage-playes are stuff'd with scarrilous, filthy, unbecomming speeches, passages, and gestures: they are the incentives, & occasions of all lust: stage-playes are the very acting of wickednesse, they are a teaching of men to be vile, and wicked. What are all your Comedies, but onely bringing the wanton lusts of men upon the stage? as if so be the hearts of men were not corrupt enough by nature , but they must needs see lewdnesse , and folly acted before their eyes, to provoke them to be wicked. Oh horrible! men are not content to be lascivious, unchaft in their thoughts, desires, and inclinations when they are at home, but they would faigne see lust acted in the life of it, they would faigne see it displayed in its colours. Is not this abominable? *Ezekiel.* 23. 14. 15. 16. *When she saw men pourtrayed upon the wall the images of the Chaldeans pourtrayed with virmilion, girded with girdles upon their loynes, exceeding in dyed attire upon their heads, all of them Princes to look to, after the manner of the Babylonians of Chaldea the land of their nativity, & as soon as she saw them with her eyes, she doted upon them, and sent messengers unto them in Caldea.* Could dead pictures do so much, a few painted images on a wall? what then will living pictures do? The

persons

Math. 5. 28.
Math. 5. 22. 23.

perfons of men acting the part of fome found, and
wanton lover, or in another habit reprefenting
the amorous looks, carriage, and deportment of
fome lewd and wanton Queane. They, when
they faw the pictures in the wall Doted on
them, and doth not the fight of luftfull amorous
fpectacles beget & ftir up luft, doth it not bewitch
and enchant the hearts of men? There are two
fad [h] examples of this in Hiftories. Befides, do not
men attire themfelves in womans habits, and is
not this a fin? *Deut. ron. 5. 22. The woman fhall not
weare that which pertaineth to a man, neither fhall a
man put on a womans garment, for all that do fo, are
an abomination to the Lord thy God.* Is there any
thing more cleare, or more expreffe? How frequent is this in ftage playes? was it not fo in the
late play, was there not one that acted a womans
part in *womans garments?* If we believe the word,
thefe were not ordinary fins, no, they are unnaturall, abominable practifes, the authors of them
are abominable, they are * *monfters* in Gods account as a learned man explaines that text.

3. The hand of God hath remarkably appeared againft the actors, and frequenters of ftage
playes. *There was a woma that went to the Theatre
to fee a play, and returned home poffeffed with an uncleane fpirit: who being rebuked in a conjuration, for
daring to affault one of the faith, that profeffed Chrift,
anfwered, that he had done well, oecaufe he had found
her upon his own ground.* Here you have the devils
own confeffion, he acknowledges ftage playes to
be finnes, he had her upon his own ground, where

he

h See D Rey-
nolds, *over-
throw of ftage
playes.* p. 51.

Prinu s Hift-
riom maftix.
p. 392. & fcy.

* *Aboinabilis
eft apud Deum
hoc eft Deus
abhorret ab
his monftrjs.
Johannes
Wolphius.* in
Deut.
*Theatre of
Gods judg-
ments.*

he would have her, and therefore he claimes a
right to do what he did. Many inftances there are
in this kind. He that hath a mind to fatisfy himfelfe may read Mr *Prin's Hiftrio-Maftix*, where
there are many Pages to this purpofe. There is
one inftance fo neere a kin to that of *Witny*, that
it may not be omitted. *Upon the* 13 *of January, An-*
no 1583. *being the Lords day, an infinite number of*
people, men, women, and children, reforted unto Paris
garden to fee Beare-baiting, playes, & other paf-times
and being all together mounted aloft upon their fcaf-
folds and galleries, and in the midft of all their jol-
lity and paftime , all the whole building (not
fo much as one ftick ftanding) fell down miraculouf-
ly to the ground. with much terror and confufion in
the fall of it; five men and two women were flaine out
right, and above one hundred and fifty perfons more
fore wounded and bruifed, whereof many dyed fhortly
after, fome of them having their braines dafhed out,
fome their heads all to quafht, fome their leggs broken
fome their armes, fome their backs, fome one hurt
fome another: there being nothing heard there, but
woefull fcreekes & cries, wch did even pierce the skies:
children there bewailng the death and hurts of their
parents, Parents of their children: wives of their Huf-
bands, and Husbands of their Wives; fo that every
way from foure of the Clock in the afternoone till
nine at night, efpecially over London *bridge; many*
were carried in and led betwixt their friends. and fo
brought home to their houfes with forrowfull heavy
hearts, like lame cripples.

4. Much more might be faid to proove the a-
bomi-

bominableneſſe of theſe playes, *from the riſe and originall of them*, they being the inventions of the Heathens, deviſed and framed on purpoſe to honour their [1] Gods withall, eſpecially *Bacchus* their Drunken God, from whence ſtage players were called *Bacchus his handy-crafts-men.* Frō the *maine ends* lookt at in them, m*ſinfull mirth and jollity.* From the ordinary *concomitants, effects, and fruits of them.* But theſe have been ſo largely handed by Dr. *Reynolds*, Mr. *Prinne*, and others, that it would be needleſſe to repeat them. There hath been ſaid enough already to prove ſtage playes to be ſinfull. And if ſo, (that we may returne to that where we left) Is it not a judgment if a man be taken in the midſt of his ſinnes? When *Nadab* & *Abihu* were ſmitten by the Lord in the midſt of their ſinnes, was it not a judgment, a ſore judgment? The ſtory you have, *Levit.* 10. 1. 2. Oh ceaſe to ſpeake againſt the God of heaven any more in this ſort. Certainly it was a judgment, and a manifeſt judgment, it was wrath from heaven, yea it was wrath from heaven againſt you in this place. Suffer me to give you this obſervation. All that were killed were the people of Witny; they were your children, your ſonnes and your daughters that were ſlaine; Why ſhould five of Witny be ſlaine outright, and not any one of other places. This Cōedy was acted in other places, but it was in *Witny* only that it proved a Tragedy. O *Witny, Witny*, the Lord is angry with thee, and

Marginal notes:

[1] Græci omnium ſuorum ludorum ſolennitatum at ꝗ adeo πάσαις δόξιας ut ait Athenæus ἢ αἰτίας εἰς ἢ Θεὸν ἀνέφερον. Sed cum veri Dei notitiam amiſerunt i-de Bacchum feſtivitaris authorem dixerunt, huic ſcenicos ludos conſecrarunt: huic dramaticam poeſin & univerſam Θεατρικὴν μουσικὴν dicarunt, quā antiquiſſimi homines eam ob cauſam προφήτας appellarunt, ſcenici hiſtriones ideo Διονυσιακοὶ τεχνῖ θ ſemper dicti. Iſaa. Caſaub. de Satyr. Græ. Poeſ. & Rom. Satyra. m E-& hilaritas there.

there are feverall fins among you, that the Lord
points out by this judgment.

1. There is the fin of Prohanenesse amongst
you, how many are there in this place, that are given only to drinking, fporting, merriments, and
paf-times? I have too fadly obferved it in paffing
the ftreets, people will fit drinking in an Ale-houfe
making themfelves merry with a Fiddle, whereas
they will not ftep over their threfhold to heare a
Sermon. Oh this is the very depth of prophaneneffe, when men care not for God, they care not
for his word, they care not for his ordinances,
they care not for the great things of falvation, but
are ftill calling for their fports and merriments,
they will be jovall and merry, that they will.

Heb. 12. 16. *Left there be any prophane perfon as
Efau,* that is an unhallowed, and unfanctifyed perfon, one that ftill lyes in his naturall filth. Why
what is the Character of fuch a one? it is added, *who
for one morfell of meat fold his birthright.* You of
this place have had the Gofpell amongft you,
Chrift and falvation is offered, heaven and happi-
neffe ftand waiting on men, few men care for this,
few men bid Chrift and falvation welcome: are
not many apt to fay, what need of all this preaching? was it not better with us when we had leffe?
Many think it much to afford one houre in a
week to heare a Sermon, but they fay, come let us
eat, and drink, and make our felves merry, let us
dance it, and card it, and be joviall whilft we may:
and I would to God there may be none fuch
found among you, that will fit up whole nights at
Cards,

Cards and Dice, that can fit day after day, many houres together in an Alehouse, that grudge a few minnutes to be spent in the service of Gcd. Oh! desperate prophaneneffe , abominable wickedneffe! the God of heaven hath revenged this prophaneneffe this day. Do but thinke with your selves, what the place was, where the hand of the Lord was seen: was it not in such a *Kind of place,* where such meetings use to bee: I speake not of that *Particular house,* but that it should be in an Inne, Taverne, or Ale-house, such a *Kind of place* to which the people of this place are so much adicted, which they haunt so much, & spend so much time in. Is there nothing to be learn'tfrom this? Doth the Lord point out nothing of the sin of this place herein ? The sinne of drunkennes is to rife & common amongst you? the drunkards are reeling in your streets, they are open and obvious, to the view of all, I my selfe have been too sad an eyewitneffe.

2. Another sin that may be feared to be amongst you is the sin of uncleanneffe. Is there no fornication, no adultery in secret corners? no such things as chambering and wantoneffe to be found amongst you? Examine well what all your songs, & carolls are, which are so often sung at your dores; & in your houses? are there none of them base, filthy, obscene. It argues too too light and wanton a spirit, that so many scores, yea some hundreds should be at a lascivious play. Oh this is a fearful sin, the sin of uncleanneffe, fornication, adultery, and those things that border on it. These

sins

fins bring aftonifhing judgments. Some fins of this
nature were they that deftroyed Sodom, and cau-
fed fire to come down from heaven upon it. *viz*:
the fin of uncleanneffe,and unnaturall lufts. Thefe
things are too fowle to be named,thefe things are
enough to make the fun in the firmament to blufh
and be afhamed, and the light of the day to hide
and couer it felfe, in which there is mention made
of fuch things.

    3.   A third fin, which is too vifible and appa-
rent,is, Neglect of the word and ordinances.Some
of them that did attend upon the ordinances have
turned their back upon them, and the generality
amongft you doe apparently fleight them. Formerly what flockinge hath there been to fer-
mons? how hath this place been filled every Al-
ley ;&corner crowded? No people fo famous for
readineffe, & diligence in hearing the word as
the people of Witny: Minifters that have occafio-
nally preached among you have obferved it, your
Name hath been famous amongft others. How
thin are your Congregations grown upo the lords
day? how fmall an handfull there are upon Lect-
ure dayes, I am to fet a witneffe? Brethren, fuffer me to fpeak my feares. I feare one of the great
fins that bath pluct down this judgment, was the
neglect of the Gofpell. It was not long fince, the
laft time that ever I preacht amongft you on the
Lords d , in a full affembly, I befeeched you, I
intreated you by all the arguments of love, gen-
tleneffe,fweetneffe, that poffibly I could to attend
upon the word. I befeecht you by the love of
God,

God, by the mercies of the Lord, by the bowells of his goodneſſe, that you would not sleight the word. The Text was from that of St. *John, God is* *love,* and the poynt from it was, *that the Love of God manifeſted to the world in the diſpenſation of himſelfe by Jeſus Chriſt, it was the moſt peereleſſe, matchleſſe, incomperable love, that ever was.* Hence were you called upon in ſuch exhortations as theſe in the Applciation. 1 Iohn:4.8,9.

Oh do not grieve ſuch a Love! doe not ſleight it! doe not abuſe it! Oh unkind ſinner! Oh hard-hearted ſinner! worſe then the blackeſt divell in hell! that canſt be drunk, that canſt ſweare, that canſt laugh at holineſſe in the face of that very Love which is come to ſave thee, to pardon thee; that hath ſent the only begotten ſonne that thou might'ſt have life through him. Do not ſin againſt this love, do not grieve it: ſuffer this love to attaine its ends, to accompliſh its deſires. The deſigne of love is to bring thee unto life, and it hath coſt it deare to bring about that deſigne, the ſonne of God muſt come downe from heaven to bring this to paſſe, and is that ſo ſmall a matter? why ſhould any of us be willing to ſtop this love in its workings, to hinder it in its aimes and intentions: all the deſigne of this love is to bring us unto life, and is there any harme in that? Ah, my Brethren, is Death ſpirituall, Eternall death, ſuch a ſweet, ſuch a pleaſant thing, that we ſhould be in love with it? Is wrath, the wrath of the Almighty, everlaſting wrath a thing to be deſired? that we ſhould refuſe to accept of the offers of eternall love, when it comes to offer life and ſalvation. With many more Reaſonings

G

in this kind. After this you were exhorted *to make use of the meanes of life and of salvation*, in some such words as these. *If you are willing to come to the Lord Jesus for life, you cannot be unwilling to attend upon those meanes, and that word, that holds forth Christ and salvation. Will any one say that that man prizes a pardon, that will not vouchsafe so much as to look upon it, nor to read it, when it is sent unto him? Oh my Brethren! the Gospell is the word of life, the word of peace, of pardon, and of salvation, can he be said to prize salvation and Christ, that will not come to that word which brings Christ, salvation, and all? Is that man willing in good earnest to be saved (however all men say they are willing, God forbid els, but is he so in good earnest?) that will not step over his threshold to heare a Sermon, where this gospell is brought, & the meās of salvation tēdred? I beseech you suffer me to speake to you in the name of the Lord; I beseech you in the name of Jesus Christ, I beseech you in the bowells of Jesus Christ, if you think this love of God the greatest love that revealeth pardō, life, happinesse, salvation, do not think it much to wait upon the word that reveales it, and makes it manifest. Faith commeth by hearing, and hearing is the ordinary meanes to beget Faith, and so to bring to Christ, and to salvation. I beseech you do not sleight this Exhortation; if you do, I must tell you, (though I am loath so to do, yet I am constrained) this Sermon will rise up in judgment against you at the last day, and I must come in as a witnesse against you.*

These were some of the arguments wher-with-all you were pressed; yet not-with-standing all these

thefe befeechings, and entreaties, to my griefe I
obferved it, fcarce were there any, that did the
more frequent the word preached, & hath not the
Lord fhewen his hand feverely? whereas there are
fcarce many Scores that wil cōe to hear the word,
the ∃ are fome Hūdreds will go to fee a wicked &
an ungodly play. Certainly the Lord hath bin aver-
ged for this. Do but read that 10. of *Lu.* frō the be
ginning & fo on, at the 5. *verfe* it is faid, *Into what-*
foever houfe you enter, firft fay, Peace be to this houfe.
but what followes? in the 10 *verfe* it is faid , *But*
into whatfoever citty ye enter, and they recieve you
not, goe your waies out into the ftreets of the fame,
and fay even the very duft of your citty which clea-
veth on us, we do wipe off againft you. And then there
is a fad clofe in v. 12. But I fay unto you that it fhall
be more tollerable for Tyre, and Sidon at the day of
judgment, then for you.

A. Another *provoking fin,* is the *fin of Athe-*
ifme, and *irreligion.* Do but read what the Lord
Jefus fpeakes to the Church of *Pergamos. Rev. 2.*
14. *I have a few things against thee,* why? what is
the matter? *Thou haft there them that hold the*
Doctrine of Balaam: and then againe at the 15. *ve.*
So haft thou alfo them that hold the doctrine of
the Nicolaitans. The doctrine of *Balaam* is expref-
fed, *He taught Balaack to caft a ftumbling block be-*
fore the children of Ifrael, to eat things facrificed
unto Idolls, and to commit fornication. The Doct,
rine of the a *Nicolaitans* was much of the fame nature, and I blufh to tell you what it was, they did
not onely hold a liberty of uncleanneffe, but a ne-

a Ου]Θ- i-
τόλμα λέγιν,
ὃτι 'ει μή τις
καθ' ἑκάστην
ὑμέραν λεγ-
γευει ζωῆς
ἢ δύναι θ με-
τέχειν τᾶ ἀ-
ωνίω.
Epiphanius
de Nicolao.

ceffity

cessity of it. Now what was the quarrell which Christ had with this church? thou haft *there* them that hold such and such things: In thee, O *Pergamos*, are found such monftrous, and abominable Doctrines, in thee are found such as maintaine the, & will ftand for them: with thee it is that they have their feat, and refidence. Are there not to be found in thee, O *Witny*, corrupt, licentious, abominable Doctrines? haft thou not alfo them, that hold them, that contend for them with might & maine? Are there none amongft you that make a mock of fin, that make fin nothing, that hold there is no fuch thing as fin? Are there none amongft you, that deny the great fundamentall Doctrines, (which are the very hinges, pillars, and foundations of all religion) denying the refurrection, the immortality of the foule, election and reprobation, Heaven and hell, that deny the damnation of any, and maintaine the falvation of all, that can take away the fcriptures, the whole Bible, and religion it felfe all at once, are there none fuch as thefe are? Thefe are fad provocations, black and difmall provocations! I would feigne believe fome poore foules are led afide through weakneffe, and fimplicity, and are beguiled through the fubtility of that old ferpent whofe wiles they are ignorant of. The good Lord deliver them, that they perifh not. Its a dangerous thing to ftumble at the fundamentalls of religion, and godlineffe, although it be through weakneffe. But *if* there be any fuch who obftinately, and pertinatioufly maintaine fuch Doctrines,

rines, againſt ceare and convincing light formerly ſhining on them, againſt the truth which ſometimes they owned and profeſſed, they are in a ſad
and fearfull caſe. Read the Epiſtles of St. *Peter, and
Jude*, and there you will ſee the ends of thoſe men
2. *Pet.* 2. 1. *They bring upon themſelves ſwift deſtruction. v.* 3. *Their Judgment now of a long time
lingereth not, and their damnation ſlumbereth not.
Ep. Iude, v.* 4. *who were before of old ordained to
this condemnation.* If a man out of deſpight make a
mock of Preaching, ſabbaths, ordinances, if there
be any worſe place in hell it is reſerved for that
man.

You ſee what the ſinnes are which are found a-
mongſt you, I have now ſhewen you your wounds,
my next work is to endeavour the healing of them,
and indeed that was my maine intention, it was
not a pleaſure to me to ſearch and lance your
your ſoares, yet that was neceſſary to a cure.

The maine exhortation preſſed on you, hath
been an exhortation to repentance, to ſerious, to
ſpeedy repentance. And that which remaines, is
to give more particular direction, what your carriage and deportment ought to be under the preſent hand of God. There are theſe foure things
you ought to ſet before you, and to have in your
eye.

1. The work of Humiliation.
2. The work of Reconciliation.
3. The work of Reformation.
4. The work of Remembrance: (for ſo it
may be called) laying it as a ſolemne charge upon

on your felves to keep in remembrance this ftrange and wonderfull providence.

1.   The firft Duty to be fet upon is the work of Humiliation. I do not meane you fhould fet up-on it in your own ftrength, but take the ftrength of Chrift with you, and the ftrength of the fpirit with you, and then you may go on.   You have finned greatly, oh humble your felves greatly be-fore the Lord! *Manaffeth* did fo after his great finnes, 2. *Chron.* 33. 12. *And when he was in af-fliction, he befought the Lord his God, and humbled himfelfe greatly before the God of his fathers.* Every particular foule fhould humble himfelfe for his particular finnes, and fay, Good Lord! what have my finnes been, that fuch wrath fhould come up-on *Witny* in my dayes! Every family fhould mourne, and lament over the finnes of that fami-ly: Hufbands fhould mourne apart, and the Wives a part, children a part, and fervants a part; every one mourning for his owne perfonall finnes, and the family finnes. In the 12. *Zachar.* 11. we read of *a great mourning,* a great mourning indeed, *as the mourning of Hadadrimmon in the valley of Megiddon.* When was that? When that good King *Iofiah* was flaine. 2. *Chron.* 35. 23. 24. 25. Oh that was a dreadfull, a terrible Judgment to have fuch a Prince taken from them! and this oc-cafioned a great mourning, the text faies, *all Iu-dah, and Ierufalem mourned for Iofiah.* All were turned mourners then, and there was no one but bare a part in thefe lamentations. *Ieremiah* the Prophet, *he lamented for Iofiah, and the finging*

men,

men, *and the singing women* spake of Iosiab in *their lamentations unto this day.* Their singing was turned into mourning, and their rejoycing into lamentation. You have had a great many singing men, and singing women in this place, such as would goe frō doore to doore singing their songs and carolls to make themselves and others mirth Oh! it were well if your singers were turned into mourners! if your harpers were turned into lamen ters!if insteed of al your songs,& carols,& dācings, you would now come and weep together, and say as *Ieremiah* doth. *Lament.* 3. 1. *How hath the Lord covered the daughter of Zion with a cloud in his anger ?* How hath the Lord covered poore *Witney* with a cloud in his anger ? and as it is in the 4. verse. *He hath bent his bow like an enemy, he stood with his right hand as an adversary, he powred out his fury like fire.* Complaine as the Church also doth in Lam. 3. with a little change in the expression. We are the people that *have seen affliction by the rod of his wrath.v.3. Surely against us is he turned, he turneth his hand all the day.v.4. our flesh, & our skin hath he made old, he hath broken our bones.* Thus I say cōe & weep together, every soule should weep, & every family should weep, & the whole Town should weep, and indeed it were well if God would put it into your hearts to keep a day of weeping, to set apart some solemne day, to fast and pray, and weep, and humble your selves before the Lord. Say unto the Lord as it is *Lam.* 1, 18. *The Lord's righteous, for we have rebelled against his commandements:* and as the Church bemoanes her selfe,

Lam:

Lam: 3: 39, 40, 41, &c. Wherefore doth a living man complaine, a man for the punishment of his sins? let us search and try our wayes, and turne again to the Lord. Let us lift up our heart with our hands unto God in the heavens. We have transgressed, and rebelled, thou hast not pardoned. Thou hast covered with anger, and persecuted us: thou hast slaine, thou hast not pittied.

2. Aime at Reconciliation. The Lord is displeased, he hath been highly provoked: oh labour to get his anger removed, and his wrath pacifyed! Run apace to the Lord Jesus, entreat him to stand betweene you, and his fathers wrath: go to, him speedily, go to him immediately, before farther wrath breake forth. It is not all our teares (though we could poure out whole rivers of thē) that can wash away one sin: no, no, *in that day* ('tis spoken immediately after the mention of that *great mourning*) *there shall be a fountaine opened for sin, and for uncleannesse.* Mourne you must, mourne greatly, mourne bitterly, yea, but it is the *fountaine* that must wash away sin, it must be the fountaine of the Lord Christs blood, that must wash away the fowle, and horrible sins of *Witney*. Come then, wash in this fountaine, wash, and you shall be cleane. In the 16 of *Numbers* we read of great wrath: no sooner had God executed that fearfull judgment upon *Korah*, and his rebellious compãy, but the people fell to murmering immediately. v. 41. *But on the morrow, all the congregation of the children of Israel murmered against Moses, and against Aaron, saying, ye have killed the peo:*
ple

Zach· 13·1.

ple of the Lord. Oh desperate, and adventrous sinners! that when they saw the judgment of God executed the very day before, yet they fell into the same sins, which they were guilty of, which had been so plagued. How angry is the Lord for this, v: 44, 45. *And the Lord spake unto Moses saying, get you up from among this congregation, that I may consume them as in a moment.* But what doth Moses do in this case? v: 46. *And Moses said unto Aaron, Take a censer, and put fire therein from off the Alter, and put on incense, and go quickly unto the congregation, and make an atonement for them, for there is wrath gone out from the Lord, the plague is begun.* This represented the mediation of Jesus Christ, who is said to *make intercession for the transgressors.* He is that *Angell* in the *Revelation,* that *stands at the Alter, having a golden censer, and much incense given to him, that he should offer it with the prayers of thee Saints. chapt.* 8. 3. Now *Moses* saies to *Aaron,* go *quickly:* or as it may be read, *make to go with speed,* that is, as the *Chaldee,* and *Greeke* translateth it, *carry quickly, or in haste.* Make haste to the Lord Jesus, away to him every soule of you: all you that have not known what the worth of the Lord Jesus is till this houre, know now how to prize him, it is he that must pacify the wrath of God that is gone out against thee for thy prophanenesse, and thine uncleannesse, and thy neglect of the word, and thine Atheisme, Oh fall in love with the incomperably pretious Lord Jesus this day, as soon as ever thou commest home fall upon thy knees & beg thou mayest have

Isa. 53.12.

ἀπεστάλθαι τ᾽

a Chrift given to thee: the wrath of the Almighty is gone out againft thee, and will otherwife certainly confume thee. There is no dealing with a fin-revenging Majefty, but only in, & by a Mediator. As for you that have intereft in this pretious Name, O make ufe of it, prefent the righteoufneffe, and fatisfaction of the Lord Jefus Chrift unto the father. It is he that muft ftand *betweene the dead, and the living*: fome are cut off already, and the wrath of the Lord is not yet appeafed. If you interpofe not the Lord Jefus, you may expect more wrath, and more plagues. This I commend to you as the chiefe, and maine direction of all the reft: it is not all thy carelefneffe, and fecurity, it is not all thy fleighting, and defpifing the judgments of God, that will be able to keep off the wrath of the Lord in the end. No, this will bring on thee fo much the more wrath, and heavyer vengeance: Get into the Lord Jefus, *hide your felves in the clefts of that rock* till this indignation be over paft. If ever Chrift be worth having, now is the time: You that cared not for Chrift when you were at eafe, and when you lived in pleafure, my thinkes you fhould long after Chrift, and be reftleffe till you have gotten him now judgment is come upon you. Oh, Brethren, if the Judgments of God in this world be fo terrible, that they are enough to abafh, and appale the ftouteft finners, how terrible, and how dreadfull will that laft, and great day of judgment bee? If thou canft not ftand before an angry God now without a Saviour, without an advocate to plead thy caufe, when

he

he doth but manifest a little of his displeasure, and gives but a gentle touch of his finger, how wilt thou stand before him without a Saviour, and an advocate ? when he shall come with millions of Saints and Angells; when the Bookes must be opened, and every mans life ripped open, and it shall be said; There waft thou drunk in such a corner, there hadst thou thy wanton dalliances upon such a bed, at such a time didst thou revile at the Ministers of God, and mock at his waies and the professors of them, so many yeares thou livedst in the world, and yet never didst study how thou mightest come to the knowledge of God, or the way to life and happinesse; when all this, and much more shall be said; and then the Lord shall not come to let in a veine of his wrath only; but he will pluck up all the sluces, & open all the floud-gates of his wrath, and vengeance when that dismall place of torment shall be set before thee, where those unquencheable flames are, where thou shalt heare the devills roaring, the damned yelling, and see all this prepared for thee, how wilt thou be able to hold up thy head at such a day ? Make sure of Christ betimes. They were the last, and dying words of one, who in his life time was the Jewell, and Paragon of Religion, and piety in the country where he lived. *Make sure of Christ.* He is better then all the gold and treasures in the world, better then the Rubies, or the Onyx stone. Thou art eternally happy if thou get him, and Eternally miserable if thou come short of him.

3. The

3. The next thing that is to be studied, and endeavoured after is Reformation. It is Reformation that the Lord looketh after. Do you think that the Lord delighteth in the death of your children? that he taketh pleasure in the breaking, bruising of your bones? is it matter of joy to him to see the hurts, and heare the dolefull complaints of your wives, servants, and neere relations? No, no, *God is love*, as you have many times heard: had not your sinnes put him upon it, there had not been so sad a spectacle found amongst you. Put away therefore that evill thing which is in the middest of you. When the children of *Israel* had fallen before their enemies, *Achan* who had taken the accursed thing, and been the occasion of the misery, and distresse that fell upon them, must be found out, and stoned. You have seene already some of the *Achans* that have troubled your peace; stone them now, and put them to death. You have heard it was the prophanenesse, the ücleannesse, the contempt of the Gospell, the Atheisme, and irreligion that is among you, that hath caused all your trouble : put away these accursed things. And here let me speake more fully to you under these foure heads.

1. To the loofer, and prophaner fort.

2. To them that formerly haue been professors, but now are fallen off.

3. To them that do still feare the Lord, and hold on in his way.

4. To all the people of the place in generall.

L. To

To the loofer, and prophaner fort, the exhortati-is, Oh put away all your drunkenneſſe, fornication, uncleanneſſe, oathes, blaſphemies; let him that was filthy be filthy no more; let him that ſtole ſteale no more: oh that you would think of lea-ving all theſe baſe, unworthy, deſperately fooliſh wayes, and think of turning to the Lord with your whole heart, and your whole foul! You that have layen rotting, and ſtinking in your luſts ma-ny yeares together, thou that art an old gray-headed ſinner, think at laſt of returning to the Lord. Ah poor creatures! what meane you? will you ruine the place you live in, and damne your own ſoules eternally? If men had but common humanity in them they would not continue in their groſſe, and hideous abominations, that would pull downe wrath upon their wives and children, friends and neighbours, the towne and place in which they live. But this is a ſmall matter in compariſon; if they had but a tender regard of their own ſoules, if they made any account of their owne ſalvation, if they had but ſo much as a prin-ciple of ſelfe-love in them, they would caſt away thoſe ſinnes, that will certainly damne them in the end. There is none of the ſinnes which thou lo-veſt ſo dearly, and huggeſt them with ſo much ten-derneſſe, and will not be brought to part with them upon any termes, (thou hadſt rather part with thy life then with ſuch a luſt) there is none of theſe thy moſt beloved ſinnes, but it will coſt thee the loſſe of everlaſting life, it will coſt thee the loſſe of God, It will coſt thee the loſſe of the

H 3. Kingdome

Kingdome of Heaven. The word fpeakes it out aloud. *No fornicator, nor Idolater, nor adulterer, nor effeminate perfon, nor theefe, nor covetuous perfon, nor drunkard, nor reviler fhall ever inherit the kingdome of God.* 1. *Cor:* 6. Poor man, doeft thou know what the Kingdome of God meaneth, from whence thou art for ever to be fhut out? or doeft thou know what that *for ever* is, which is the line and meafure of thy torments? Sit downe, and paufe a while, and think what eternity is: thy life is but a minnute, a dreame, a fhaddow, it is gone before thou think of it: count over the houres of the day, and is the day fo long a thing, it is but the running of a few fuch, and then there is a period fet to all thy pleafures. How quickly mayeft thou on thy death-bed look over all thy life paft, and account it as a very little thing, as a meer point, and beginning only of that which is life? but canft thou look beyond eternity? canft thou conceive when everlaftingneffe will have an end? all thy pleafures are gone and paffed, they are paffed over as in a dreame, and now thou art in the midft of eternity before thou art aware. How fearfull then will thefe thoughts be: what muft I be *ever* thus? Muft I be tormented in thefe flames without end? Is there no hope, no poffibilities of being otherwife then I am? After I have fuffered fo many millions of yeares; is there *for ever* ftill behind? Try a little in thine owne thoughts, and fee where thou canft put bonds, and limits to that which is *for ever.* Try where thou canft put a ftop, beyond which thou canft think of no more: is it better to

be

be everlaftingly happy, or everlaftingly miferable after a fcore for two of yeares? Think of thefe things, I befeech you by all the calls, mercies, judgments of the Lord, by all the riches of his patience, forbearance, long-fuffering exercifed towards you. Oh do not put off the thoughts of thefe things, Do not any more *chufe abominable things which his foule hateth. Seek ye the Lord, while he may be found, call ye upon him while he is neer. Let the wicked forfake his way, and the unrighteous man his thoughts: and let him returne unto the Lord, and he will have mercy upon him, and to our God, for he will abundantly pardon.*

2. To thofe that have forfaken their former profeffion, the exhortation to them is, O Returne, Returne to the good old way of God, returne to the ordinances, returne to the ufe and exercife of holy duetyes, to the ufe of prayer, confeffion of fin, and the like: if you do not, fearfull will your Judgment be. I hope fome of them that are gone aftray do belong to the Lord, but truly you muft come back by weeping-croffe.

I could tell you fad ftoryes in this kind. I fpeak not by heare-fay: I have knowen them that have fmarted deeply for fleighting the ordinances, neglecting prayer, for low and undervaluing thoughts of Chrift and his bloud. I could tell you of fome, that living under fuch a temptation but for a week, or two, in that fhort time had loft all their former communion with God, and being delivered from the fnare accounted their recovery as a

new

new converſiõ. The experience of one in this kind was ſo eminent, that I thought I was bound to make it publick, that it might ſerve to ſtop, and reſtraine them which are ſo prone to apoſtacy in the preſent age, and I ſhall ſet it down, as neer as I can, in the ſame words and expreſſions, as I had it frõ the perſons own hand. *Being not well eſtabliſhed, I was ſoon drawn away in my hearte, ſecretly to decline frõ that good old way which formerly I walked in, I heard one upon* Juſtification, *and* Chriſts *comming in the fleſh,* & upon that place, Chriſt in you the hope of glory, *in ſuch a manner as I never heard the like before, that I was ſtruck with amazement with the manner of his plauſible ſpeech. And having heard a good report of the man, and had ſome experience before that he was an able mã to miniſter comfort to them that were in diſtreſſe, I was exceedingly taken with what came from him. And in his poynt of* Iuſtification, *he did labour to beat off from repentance, and from confeſſion of ſin, or begging of pardon for ſin, and held it out, that theſe were a calling in queſtion the faithfullneſſe of God; for he ſhewed that all that the* Saints *had to do, was to beleeve, and render prayſe; and as he ſayd, he ſpake his owne experience, that he had found more of God in one dayes walking in beleeving, then in many yeares in walking in that ſtrict courſe of praying, and faſting, and keeping dayes of humiliation, and blamed thoſe* Miniſters *that did hold forth ſuch doctrines. Theſe things he backed on with ſuch* Arguments, *that it did take much upon the affections of them that heard him. For I never heard him pray, but he would*
ſometimes

sometimes give thanks and that so sweetly, that it
did even ravish the soules of them that heard him
and did much presse on to that duty.

Thus hearing him at severall times, by degrees I
fell from the good old wayes I was trained up in by
my parents, and especially that which God had taught
me by faithfull Ministers, and soone was I poysoned
with that Doctrine, which my corrupt nature did soone
close with; to the great dishonour of the pretious Gospell, to the grieving of the good spirit of God, and the
wounding of mine owne conscience, which was not
soon healed. I began to try conclusions with God, and
and walked as a loose libertine, and cast of the duty
of prayer to God in private, and so quickly I lost my
communion with God, and he withdrew himselfe from
me, and left me for a time : and no sooner had God left
me, but Satan came in with his delusions, and formed
himself into an Angel of light, and carryed me up into a fooles Paradise, and lulled me asleep in security,
and carryed me on in that condition for the space of
an yeare and halfe before the Lord awakened me.
And no sooner had I left seeking of God in private,
but the Lord left me to publique shame; for my heart,
and strength was let out in an eager persuit of the
world, and love of the creatures, and a fearfull sleighting of the Sabbath, which began to be a burthen to me,
and I had an odious sleighting esteeme of the Ministers of God, and questioned their judgments in hold-
ing forth the word to the people, and I was exceedingly perplexed with vaine thoughts, and by degrees
led into such thoughts as I am ashamed to name, and
by this the Lord awakened me, for I was exceedingly

I

startled

startled at it, and began to consider with my self, that
I was out of Gods way, and therefore out of Gods pro-
tection. Then I began to remember from whence I was
fallen, but it was long ere I could do my first workes,
but I was resolved to turne to my first husband, for
then it was better with me then now. But I found it
a hard pluck before I found my God a reconciled father, pardoning my sin of Apostacy, though I sought it
with bitter teares for the space of halfe an yeare. And
I thought to have kept it to my selfe, and none should
have knowen my trouble, but the anguish of my spirit
was so exceeding great, that I could not hide it from
God or man, for I was afraid the Lord would have
made me a publick example to all that knew me, and
that I should have been quite distracted, and ran a-
bout the streets like one of those that children run after. But when I saw there was no remedy, I made
my case knowen, and got all the helpes I could to seek
God for me. When I made my approach to God I was
beaten back by mine adversary, and by mine owne accusing conscience, which was more to me then a thousand witnesses: And often those words were sound-
ing in mine eares. Him that draweth back my soule
abborreth, and he that putteth his hand to the plough
and looketh back, is not fit for the kingdom of heaven,
and woe to you Scribes, and Pharises hypocrites, and
that in the 6.of the Hebrews, them that have tasted of
the good word of God, and the powers of the world to
come, if they fall away, it is impossible to renew them
by repentance, with many more places: and when I
would have prayed in private, it was told me that God
would not heare me, then I replyed that I hoped God
would

would *heare him that sate at his right hand, but it was replyed to me againe the Lord had said to him,* (*as he had to* Jeremiah) *pray not for this people, I was so lamentably tortured, I could not sleep, nor eat, nor take any contentment in any relation I had, and had not the Lord witheld me from that which the devill tempted me unto, I had surely ended my life.* So low was this poore soule brought, and so deep was the diftreffe in which the Lord left it before it was recovered: & indeed I cānot declare all, leaft this relation fhould feeme too tedious. But it pleafed the Lord at laft mercifuly to recover this poor diftreffed foule, though it were long firft, (that I may ufe fome of its own expreffions) *before the Lord did feale unto it its pardon, many a bitter day, and night it did undergoe:* & to this very day it makes fad, & heavy complaints, & undergoes many a fharp conflict, but the Lord is pleafed to fanctify thefe and former difpenfations in fuch a way as that there are few Chriftians in which there is fo much humility, mortifyedneffe, fuch fweet breathings after God, fuch high prizings of his prefence, and humble attendance on the ordinances, & frequent ufe of holy duetyes to be found.

So famous an inftance as this is might ferve to poyfe, and ballance the loofe and ficle fpirits of fuch who begin to hang off from, & to be indifferent unto the good waies of God. Beware of Apoftacy. Apoftacy is a fearfull fin, it is the high way to the fin againft the Holy Ghoft, *that fin which fhall never be pardoned in this world or in the world to some.* Take heed how you medle with edge-

I 2   tooles,

tooles, as the proverbe is . *Whoever falls on this stone it will grind him to powder.* Who ever shall clash with the great FundamentallDoctrines, the Doctrines about sin, whether there be any such thing yea or no, touching the resurrection, Heaven, hell, the last Judgment, he that shall play, and dally with these things, and take liberty to speak for them or against them, such wantonnesse as this is will proove his ruine in the end . Did you not once believe these things? were they not once Articles of your faith? how is it that you come to cast them off? Oh it is the most dangerous thing in the world for a man to be medling, and tampering with, and at last come to a flat downright denying of the great fundamentall truths of religion, the things which sometimes he beleeved and professed the beleife off ! this man is in a faire way to the unpardonable sin: I do not say this is that sin, but he that is come to this had need look to himself, he is in the way thereunto without abundance of mercy to recover him. Much have those to answer for, and fearfull is their Judgment like to be, who peremptorily, and obstinately maintaine such desperate opinions, that all men shall be saved alike, that sin is nothing, but only that men make it something by their own Melancholly fancies, and timerous apprehentions.[b] This is the very Bane, and cut-throat of all religion, this is that which cuts the very sinewes of Godlinesse, this is that which undermines the worship of God in the world, and plucks it up by the very rootes. Take away the name, and notion of sin, make it

nothing

[b] Ἀ δὴ (repete ex superioribis τὸ μὴ ὅτι ὡς ἢ) θεὸν, ἢ ὄντα μὴ προνοεῖν ἢ προνοοῦντα μὴ ἀγαθὸν ᾗ), καὶ δίκαιον) ᾗ παντοδαπῆς ἀδικίας ὅτι συνεκπικώτατα, καὶ πρὸς πᾶσαν κακίαν συνωθοῦντα τῇ τῆς εἰλωκότα δοξάσμασιν. ὡς γὸ ἡ εὐσέβεια μήτηρ τῶν ἀρετῶν ἀρετάνη, ἔτω καὶ τάπης κακίας ὑγμῶν ἡ τῆς εὐσεβείας ἀπόπτωσις. Hierocl.

nothing, who then will regard to worſhip, feare, obey the great God? who will care for any of his commands? Do you not think the Lord is *jealous* for theſe things? Brethren, my heart will hardly ſerve me to ſpeake of theſe things, its even rea- dy to dye, and ſink within me. Good Lord! what wilt thou doe for thy great Name? how poor? how ſleight? how contemptible a thing do men make of thee in the world? men begin to forget that they are thy creatures, and that thou haſt made them! I could even here break forth into teares, and ſay. *Oh that my head were waters and mine eyes a foun- taine of teares that I might weep day, and night* for the diſhonour, ſcorne, and contempt that iscaſt vpon the bleſſed God by theſe things.

It is time for the *Angells* of the Churches, the Mi- niſters, and Meſſengers of Jeſus Chriſt to carry that peece of the *everlaſting Goſpell, and to preach unto them that dwell on earth, and to every nation, and kindred, and tongue, and people, ſaying with a loud voice: Feare God, and give glory to him, worſhip him that made heaven, and earth, and the ſea, and the fountaines of water.* It was ſaid in *Athanaſius* his time, that the world was become an *Arrian,* and now it may be ſayed that the world beginnes to turne *Atheiſt.* Some there are that dare pro- feſſe it. One upon that paſſage: *The foole hath ſaid in his heart, there is no God,* was not afraid to utter ſuch words, *That foole ſpake the truth.* Oh monſter! eternity will be a thing long enough to torment thee, and make thee feele whether there be a God yea, or no. But it is not all thy blaſphe-

A briefe addition touching Atheiſme.

Revel. 14. 6.7.

I 3 my

my can rid thee of thy folly. Canſt thou produce
the records of the world for ſix, or ſeaven thouſand yeares agoe? canſt thou confute the book
of Geneſis, and bring to light ſomewhat more
ancient, and authentique then it ? Canſt thou tell
who was Adams Father ? and what the generations of men were before him?riſe up as high in thy
thoughts as thou canſt,wilt thou not at laſt come to
ſome firſt man? was this man made yea, or no?who
was it that made him? was it himſelf ? then he was
before himſelfe, but was he made by ſome other ?
who was that ? or was he from everlaſting? why
then doth he not continue to everlaſting? will any
thing deſtroy it ſelfe? Durſt thou truſt thine own
ſenſe? are there any ſuch things as ſpirits? if not;
why are there ſo many wretched creatures ſuffer
for their familiar converſe with them? if thou do
believe that there are ſuch things as evill ſpirits,
who is it that keepes thē in order,& ſetts bounds
to their mallice? But ſuch mōſters who deny the
Principles of their being ſhould be rather hiſſed out
ofthe world with abhorrence,thē diſputed againſt.

　　As there are many that dare *profeſſe Atheiſme*,
ſo there are many that durſt *live* it. How pe-
remtory and reſolved are men in wayes of ſin?how
light a thing do they make of the word commands and threats of God, and of every thing
thing that might keep them in awe, and retaine
them in their obedience to their acknowledge-
ment, and obſervance of the great God? Men begin to think they are above the word, above hell
above damnation,and in effect above God. What
a poor, and contemptible thing is religion grown
　　　　　　　　　　　　　　　　　　in

in the world? Certainly, if religion be the keeping of an awe of God upon a mans spiritt, the religation, and binding of the soule over to him, the conftant obfervance of him, and ftrict conformity to his will, there is little of this religion to be found in the world.

In all thefe refpects it becommeth the fervants of the Lord to beftirre themfelves, to contend zealoufly for God, for the caufe of religió, and not patiently to fuffer the name of God, his worfhip, religion it felfe to dye, and be forgotten in the thoughts, & lives of men

3. To you that feare the Lord, and walk on in his wayes, the exhortation to you is, be more holy, be more humble, be more heavenly minded, be more fruitfull in good workes: *Zeph. 2, 3. Seek ye the Lord, all ye meek of the earth which have wrought his Judgment, feek righteoufneffe, feek meekneffe.* Ye that are meek already, feek more meekneffe, ye that have wrought righteoufneffe, be more righteous, and abound in all the fruits of righteoufneffe.

The Lords eye *is* more efpecially fet upon you, he obferves in a more peculiar manner what your carriage will be, the Lord expecteth you fhould not onely mourne for your own finnes, but for the finnes of the place in which you live. Brethren, me thinkes there is not that growth amongft you which I could wifh, I could be glad to fee more life, more fweet breathings after God amongft you. Me thinkes you do not love God, and the Lord Jefus Chrift enough, you difcourfe of him but feldome, and fpeak of him but coldly. *Ignatius* had his heart fo inflamed with

with the love of Chrift, that when he fpake of him, he would fay , *My love was crucifyed.* Some are fo full of love to him, as that they are ravifhed when they think of him, they break out, and fay, oh that excellent! that incomperable one how preti-ous is the Lord Jefus! how pretious is he! Men, and Angels are too little to love him, and admire him. For the Lords fake ftirre up your felves, entertaine Chrift better , and entertaine the Gofpell better. When the Gentiles heard, that the Gofpell was fent to them, and thatit appertained to them as well as to the Jewes, it is faid, *they were glad, and glori-fyed the word of the Lord. Acts.* 13. 48. Oh this was wellcome newes, joyfull tidings to them indeed! their hearts were even ravifhed , and tranfported with fuch bleffed tidings as thefe, that Chrift fhould become *falvation* to them, as well to the Jewes, for that was it which was made knowen to them in *v.* 47. *They glorifyed the word,* they magnifyed, and advanced the word. Oh this was the beft word that ever they heard! an excellent, and a fweet word! I befeech you, my brethren, ftirre up your felves, *and provoke one another to love, and to good workes.* It is a great fault in the profeffors of this place, that they maintaine fuch a diftance, and ftrangeneffe one towards another. The ancient Saints *fpake often one to another. Malachy:* 3. 16. The Primitive Saints in the Apoftles times met of-ten, they prayed together, and conferred together. So it fhould be with you, you fhould be often vifi-ting one another, and afking each other, Oh my Friend! what are your temptations? what are

your

your comforts? what have the dealings of God
been with your spirit since we mett laft? is
grace kept alive? or is it more dead? This is the
way to be a thriving people. I would faine that
you of this place fhould be patternes to all that
are round about you for humility, for heavenly-
mindedneffe, for foundneffe in the faith, for experience, for holineffe.

4. To all in generall, the Exhortation is, Labour
to fet up religion in this place, fet it up in your
hearts, fet it up in your families, fet it up, as much
as may be, in the whole towne. Away now with all
your finfull fports, and merriments, away with all
your cards, and dice, finging, dancing, and fuch
like vanityes. Infteed of thefe things fet up Cate-
chizing, praying in the family morning, and eve-
ning, and let one neighbour come to another, and
fay, come let us go to heaven together, and feek
the Lord together. *Jerem.* 50, 4. 5. *In thofe dayes,
and in that time faith the Lord, the children of Ifrael fhall come, they, and the children of Judah together, going & weeping: they fhall go, & feek the Lord
their God. They fhall ask the way to Zion with their
faces thitherward faying, come, and let us joyne our
felves to the Lord in a perpetuall covenant that fhall
not be forgotten.* Oh what a bleffed change would
this bee, if young, and old, rich, and poor, hufbands, and wives, parents, and children, mafters,
and fervants would all joyne together; if they
would come *weeping* together, and *feek* the Lord,
if all the people in this place would fet their faces
towards *Heaven,* and toward *Religion,* and fay,

K   come

Come let us joyne our selves in a perpetuall Covenant, we will strike in with the Lord this day,
and we will never alter our choice more, it shall
be a *Covenant that shall never be forgotten.* If you
would all resolve this day, Come, we will goe to
Zion with our faces thitherward. We will go where
the word is preached, and where the ordinances
are set up, and where the worship of God is cele-
brated, oh we will neglect the word no more, & we
will neglect the ordinances no longer. This is one
of the last requests I have to leave with you, oh do
not neglect the opertunityes of hearing the word,
and comming to the Ordinances as you have done
For the Lords sake, you that are masters of families come your selves, and bring your children, and
servants along with you; you that have friends,
bring your friends with you. Go weeping (as they
did) and say, oh we have neglected the word,
and neglected Christ, and neglected salvation, but
we will neglect them no more. Let that prophecy
be fulfilled of you which was spoken, *Isai.2.3. And
many people shall goe, and say, Come ye, and let us goe
up to the mountaine of the Lord, to the house of the
God of Jacob, and he will teach us of his wayes, and
we will walk in his paths, for out of Zion shall goe
forth the Law, and the word of the Lord out of Jeru-
salem.* Redeeme an houre in the week day to heare
the word, your callings will not prosper ever the
worse.

4, The last thing I have to propound to you
by way of direction, is the Duty of Remembrance.
Forget not the Wonderous workes which the
Lord

Lord hath wrought. When mercyes, or Judgements are new, and fresh, we are apt to speak of them, and to be affected with them, but a little time weares them out of our minds, and blots them quite out of our Remembrance. Oh take heed of this. *Bind* this sad Providence *for a signe upon your* hands, and let it *be as Frontlets between your eyes.* Set it down in your *Almanacks,* and keep a Regifter of the Day: oh this was the black, and difmall day of Gods vifitation on poor *Witny.* It were good if you kept fome folemne day every yeare as a remembrance of this fad, and heavy ftroke. For as great mercyes' require great, and and folemne praifes, fo do great judgments require great, aed folemne humiliation. *They fpeake of Jofiah in their lamentations to this day, and made them an Ordinance in Ifrael:* and *behold they are written in the Lamentations.* 2. *Chron.* 35. 25. It feemes they had a conftant remembrance of that judgment (the loffe of good *Jofiah*) they fpeak of him *to this day.* It was a conftant practife amongft them to remember that fad ftroke: and they had a folemne Book of Lamentations appointed to mourne for this judgment. *Luke.* 17, 32. *Remember Lots wife.* We have not many fuch *Remembers* in all the Book of God upon fo fpeciall an occafion, (they may eafily be all reckoned up) and therefore here is fome fpeciall thing hinted to us. Here was a fpeciall monument of Gods judgment on a woman that was hankering after her old pleafures, fhe had been ufed to the delights, and contentments of *Sodom,* and fhe was

loth

loath to part with thefe: fhe lookt back to the *Sodom* of her former pleafures, and contentments, and whilft fhe is looking back fhe became a *Pillar offalt.* Oh remember this, (faith our Saviour) *Remember Lots Wife.* There is an accent put on this. You of this place have been hankering after fports, and merriments, you have been mightily fet on thefe things, and the Lord hath fhewen his difpleafure by an Eminent hand, and a ftreched out arme. Oh remember this, remember the Tragicall ftory at the *White Hart.*

You have heard now at large what your duty is; in generall it is to fall upon the work of Repentance. You have likewife been directed particularly how to carry your felves in that work; and what the particular Duetyes are which are to be done by you, and what the Lord expects from each of you in your feverall rankes, and places. That which remaines is only, in the clofe of all, to adde a motive, or two (to that which hath been already faid) to preffe that which is your duety on you.

1. If you do not repent, fome worfe thing will come upon you. It may be the Lord may fend a Fire next to confume all your houfes; it may be he may fend the peftilence among you to devoure you, or if not that, a famine: the Lord hath wayes enough to punifh unrepentant finners. Read over that 26. of *Leviticus,* & there you will fee what the Lord threatens in fuch a cafe, *v.*23.24. *If ye will not be reformed by thefe things, but will walk contrary unto me: then will I alfo walk contrary unto you, and will*

will punish you yet feaven times for your finnes. v. 27
And if ye will not for all this hearken unto me, but
walk contrary unto me: then I will walk contrary un-
to you alfo in fury; and I, even I, will chaftife you fea-
ven times for your finnes. If you think to wax ftout
and ftubborne againft the Lord, he will be as ftout
againft you, if you walk contrary to him he will
doe fo to you, and if one judgment will not do it,
he will follow you with a fecond, & a third, and if
you ftill harden your hearts againft him, he will
cōe againft you in *Fury,* he will fummon up all his
wrath , and vengeance, and if he be able to break,
and ruine you, to be fure he will do it. Oh it is a
dreadfull word. *v.* 17. *I will fet my face againft*
you, and that in the 28. *verfe. I, even I will chaftife*
you. As much as if he fhould fay, I the great God,
I that made heaven, and earth, and can turne the
foundation of it upfidedown whē I pleafe, I will fet
my felfe againft you, I will engage all my wifedōe,
and all my power, I will put forth all my glory,
and excellency to deftroy you.

If temporall judgments will not prevaile, God
hath eternall punifhents in a readineffe for obfti-
nate, and incorrigible finners. *Tophet is prepared,*
&c. Hell is in readineffe, eternall flames, ever-
lafting burnings are prepared; and thofe that
would not be tamed, and brought into order by
the judgments of God in this world, will be ftill
and calme enough when they are thrown there.
Then thy pride and ftoutneffe of heart againft the
Lord, thy ftubbornneffe, and incorrigibleneffe
will do thee little good. This hath God prepared,

Pf,

Pf. 7. 11, 12, 13. God is angry with the wicked eva-
ry day: if he turne not, he will whet his fword, he
hath bent his bow, and made it ready ; he hath alfo
prepared for him the inftruments of death. Are not
the judgments of God in this world terrible e-
nough? do they not ftrike deep enough? do men
beare up themfelves againft the Almighty, and
wax proud againft him notwithftanding thefe?Oh!
he hath yet a deadly inftrument left behind, he
can ftrike them into hell, and then they are ftruck
to purpofe. Art thou not afraid of the firft death,
(the worft as thou fuppofeft of temporall evills)
becaufe that is but a fhort paffage? But there is
the fecond death, when thou fhalt be ever dying,
and yet never dye: thou fhalt be alwayes in the
pangs, and agonyes of death,and yet never paft
death it felfe. *The judgments of God in this world*
they are but as the Alphabet, as the A. B. C. to that
great, and laft judgment. It was *Luthers* expreffion.
Oh how great (fayes he againe) *fhall that*
confiftory be, When the Divine majefty fhall appeare,
and fo many thoufand Angels and by how much the
greater the Majefty of that court fhall be, fo much
greater will the dread, and horror be that will fall
upon wicked men.

2. If you be a reformed people, the Lord will
delight in this place, as much as ever he hath loa-
thed it. *The Lord doth not afflict willingly,nor grieve*
the children of men. No, Judgment is his ftrange
work; had you not put him to it, he had never
done that which he hath,

Returne now un*to* the Lord make a covenant
with

O quantum e-
rit iftud Con-
fiftorium ,quod
Majeftate di-
vinâ apparen-
te, & tot mil-
libus Angelo-
rum celebrabi-
tur, & quanto
majoris Ma-
jeftatis,tanto
majoris terro-
ris,& horroris
erit impiis.
Luth.

with him. this day to ſerve him with a per-
fect heart, and a willing mind. Chooſe the Lord
for your God, and give up your ſelves in Chriſt
Jeſus to him, to walk with him unto all wellplea-
ſing, then will he rejoyce over you to do you good
he will ſet himſelfe to bleſſe you with his whole
heart, and with his whole ſoule, *Bleſſed* ſhall you
be in the *towne, bleſſed in the field, bleſſed in your
basket, and bleſſed in your ſtore. Bleſſed when you
riſe up, and bleſſed when you lye down.* All the people that paſſe by you ſhall ſay. Behold *Witny,* the
Place which the Lord hath bleſſed. The Lord ſhal
take away your reproach, and it ſhall no more be
ſaid, this is *Witny,* whom the the Lord hath plagued, but this is *Witny* whom the Lord hath loved, whom the Lord delighteth in. Yea, the Lord
himſelfe ſhall *Bleſſe you out of Zion.* You ſhall have
all the Goſpell mercyes, knowledge ſhall increaſe,
and the feare of the Lord abound amongſt you:
others ſhall bee provoked by your zeale, they
ſhall come, and ſee the religion that is in *Witny,*
and ſay: Behold the place that was eminent for *ſin,*
and *judgment,* is now become eminent for *Holineſſe, and mercy.* And now I may ſay as *Moſes* did,
after he had thundered out all the curſes, and
ſweetly laid forth all the bleſſings of the Lord upon their obedience or diſobedience to the Law, *I
have ſet life, and death before you this day.* Oh chuſe
the way of life, and you are bleſſed, bleſſed ſhall
you be here, and bleſſed for evermore.

FINIS